Morocco

Morocco

TEXT BY *Paul Bowles*

PHOTOGRAPHS BY *Barry Brukoff*

Harry N. Abrams, Inc., PUBLISHERS

Editor: Robert Morton
Designer: Robert McKee

Library of Congress Cataloging-in-Publication Data
Bowles, Paul, 1910–
Morocco / text by Paul Bowles ; photographs by Barry Brukoff.
p.   cm.
ISBN 0–8109–3631–3
I. Morocco—Description and travel. 2. Morocco—Pictorial works.
I. Brukoff, Barry.   II. Title.
DT310.2.B68   1993
964—dc20   93–20181
                                                      CIP

Published in 1993 by Harry N. Abrams, Incorporated, New York
A Times Mirror Company

Printed and bound in Hong Kong

CONTENTS

ACKNOWLEDGMENTS *Barry Brukoff*

I wish to dedicate this book to the Davis sisters; my mother Edna and my aunt Isabelle.

I would like to acknowledge and thank the following people, each of whom has made a significant contribution to this book:

Paul Bowles for kindly agreeing to collaborate on this project;

Ned Leavitt for assisting me in bringing this project to fruition in many ways, not the least of which was finding Mr. Bowles in Tangiers;

Driss Britel of the Moroccan Government Tourist Office for providing invaluable assistance and information throughout my travels in Morocco;

David Travis and Ray Young who are responsible for producing the color prints for sale through myself and my gallery exhibitions;

Heather Graef for her aid in communicating my vision of this book to my publisher;

Robert Morton and Robert McKee of Harry N. Abrams.

The film for this project was generously donated by the Professional Imaging Division of Eastman Kodak Company.

Readers may wish to know the equipment used to make these photographs: Nikon FE2 and 8008 camera bodies, and Nikkor lenses ranging from 20mm to 200mm.

Meknès—courtyard of the mosque containing the tomb of Moulay Ismael

INTRODUCTION

Geographical distances can be dealt with: Mount Erebus and Easter Island are both far away, but eventually reachable. Temporal distance, on the other hand, even its shortest span, cannot be overcome. Yesterday is unattainable save in imagination.

To aid the reader's imagination in its task of seizing the essence of how things were but no longer are, and of how they are now, it is important that a chronicler adhere to a scrupulous honesty in reporting. Any conscious distortion is equivalent to cheating at solitaire: the purpose of the game is nullified. The account must be as near to the truth as he can get, and it seems to me that the surest way to achieve that is to aim for precision in describing his own reactions. A reader can get an idea of what a place is really like only if he knows its effects upon someone of whose character he has some idea, of whose preferences he is aware. Thus it seems essential that the writer place a certain insistence upon the objective presentation of his own personality; it provides an interpretive gauge with which the reader can measure for himself the relative importance of each detail, like the scale of miles in the corner of a map.

It goes without saying that whatever attempts have been undertaken to make a place accessible to the visitor are just so many barricades in the way of the writer, and if he manages to make contact with the place it will be in spite of them rather than thanks to them. The purpose of official aid for the foreign visitor is to make individual research unnecessary; in many countries there is a further, more sinister design in government-sponsored tourist bureaus: a conscious intent to discourage personal relationships between strangers and residents. Writers are particularly suspect, as is natural, but it is one of their routine tasks to circumvent this sort of thing.

The texts which follow were accurate enough at the time of writing, but clearly many factual statements no longer apply, for example: prices, even lengths of time required to get from one place to another. Reference is made to regular sailing of passenger ships between Europe and the United States. How could I have guessed that within a very short time the only means of travel would be by air? Had I been told in 1972 that I should never again be able to go back and forth to New York by ship, I should have ridiculed that statement as a science-fiction prophecy of doom.

Inevitably there are many discrepant details to be noted in a comparison of the way things were forty years ago with the way they are now. This is particularly true in a rapidly evolving society such as that of Morocco. Apart from the fundamental difference made by the shift from colonial management to political independence, the myriad changes are largely superficial, leaving the basic nature of the society much as it was before the introduction of motorized vehicles and television.

The Moroccans, traditionally renowned for their hospitality toward foreigners, remained tranquil during the Gulf War, despite their overwhelming support of Iraq. I doubt that the majority here were ever aware that King Hassan had despatched a military contingent to help the United Nations to subdue Saddam. I was here, leading my usual daily life during that time of tension, and nothing occurred. People knew I was an American, but no one alluded to my nationality as I walked in the street. There was no visible change toward foreigners in the attitude of the populace. Yet although everyone was deeply affected by the knowledge that an "innocent" Moslem nation was being destroyed by infidel forces, the violent reaction that might have been expected did not appear.

One aspect of this part of the world which has not changed in the sixty years I've known it is the beauty of the landscape. I can think of nothing more stimulating than to embark, preferably in a convertible, on a long, unhurried voyage through the wild Moroccan countryside, following the roads where they lead, beside the streams that cut through the mountains and across the empty stretches of desert. The highways were built wide and graded to

Marrakesh—doorway of the Villa Majorelle

accommodate the French military vehicles and tanks. No signboards mar the splendid vistas. Even so, the *pistes*, or trails, are more satisfying, for they go to places whose existence is still unexpected by the tourist. And, for that matter, equally unsuspected by the Moroccans placed in the official tourist bureaus to advise foreigners how to proceed in their travels. These men know all about the big cities—there are only five in all: Casablanca, Rabat, Marrakesh, Fez and Meknès—and the hotels to be found in them. But, they tell you, they can't be expected to have information regarding the state of the roads in the Djebel Sarrho, or whether as a result of attacks by the Polisario in the farther reaches of the Anti Atlas, the region has been shut off by the military. Sometimes the southern section of the Dran Valley is open to motorists who hope to make trips by camel through the oasis beyond M'hamid, and sometimes it is closed. The only way to find out whether this is possible is to go all the way to Zagora and see what conditions are to the south of there. One grows accustomed to living in a state of constant uncertainty. What you can count on, if you are in a region that is at all inhabited and your car fails to ford a river or you find the road blocked by boulders, is that someone will arrive and do his best to help you. If need be, he will run off and return with all the men and boys of the nearest hamlet, who will do everything within their power to solve your difficulty.

Of the five large cities mentioned above, Casablanca is not a Moroccan city and never was one; it was invented by the French. Rabat, were it not full of embassies and consulates and if it did not contain the palace housing the king and his family, would be of scant interest. Meknès under the French

Beni Mellal—a view of the old fort

was the seat of the wine industry, considerably interfered with at the time of Moroccan independence (1956). Its similarity, as well as its proximity, to Fez makes a comparison inevitable, with Meknès the loser. The city reached a certain grandeur under the ferocious Moulay Ismail. Now one could call it a poor man's Fez. The only two cities worth staying in and observing are Fez and Marrakesh. Marrakesh is a huge, wide-open market. The alleys in the medina are full of strangers come down from the mountains and up from the desert. Outside the medina the streets, wide and straight, lead off into the flat distance. It's a city open to the sky. The earth, walls and buildings are all of a uniform color, a shade somewhere between tomato bisque and old rose. The French posters always referred to "Marrakech la Rouge," just as those they produced to attract visitors to Fez spoke only of "Fèz la Mystérieuse." In the latter case they were accurate: undeniably Fez gives the impression of a city folded in upon itself, intent on hiding whatever it contains from the inquisitive gaze of the outsider. At this moment in time, Fez is unique in the world. Its two erstwhile rivals, Damascus and Tunis, have undergone modernizing work that removes them from competition with Fez as medieval monuments.

It may be that my eulogy of travel through the Moroccan countryside has no place in a work devoted primarily to what is in the cities. This comes from one who has always been more deeply moved by the works of nature than by those of man. In this instance, however, the works of man are worthy of the most careful scrutiny.

Volubilis—ruins of the first century Roman city.

THE WORLDS OF TANGIER

In the summer of 1931, Gertrude Stein invited me to stay a fortnight in her house at Bilignin, in southern France, where she always spent the warm months of the year. At the beginning of the second week she asked me where I intended to go when I left. Not having seen much of the world, I replied that I thought Villefranche would be a good place. She was gently contemptuous. "*Anybody* can go to the Riviera," she declared. "You ought to go somewhere better than that. Why don't you try Tangier?" I was hesitant, and explained that living there might cost more than my budget allowed me. "Nonsense," she said. "It's cheap. It's just the place for you."

A week later I was aboard a little ship called the *Imaréthie II* bound for various North African ports, and ever since I have been grateful to Gertrude Stein for her intelligent suggestion. Beginning with the first day and continuing through all the years I have spent in Tangier, I have loved the white city that sits astride its hills, looking out across the Strait of Gibraltar to the mountains of Andalucia.

In those days Tangier was an attractive, quiet town with about 60,000 inhabitants. The medina looked ancient, its passageways were full of people in bright outlandish costumes, and each street leading to the outskirts was bordered by walls of cane, prickly pear and high-growing geranium. Today, where this thick vegetation grew, are the cracking façades of new apartment houses; the Moslems have discarded their frogged Oriental jackets and enormous trousers of turquoise, orange, pistachio or shocking pink, to don Levis, and secondhand raincoats imported by the bale from America; the population has augmented at least threefold, and I'm afraid the city would never strike a casual visitor as either quiet or attractive. There must be few places in the world which have altered visually to such an extent in the past quarter of a century.

A town, like a person, almost ceases to have a face once you know it intimately, and visual modifications are skin-deep; the character is determined largely by its inhabitants, and a good deal of time is required to change their attitudes and behavior. Tangier can still be a fascinating place for the outsider who has the time and inclination to get acquainted with its people. The foreigner who lives here on a long-term basis will still find most of the elements which endeared the place to him in the old days, because he knows where to look for them. Tangier is still a small town in the sense that you literally cannot walk along a principal street without meeting a dozen of your friends with whom you must stop and chat. What starts out to be a ten-minute stroll will normally take an hour or more.

You will run into a Polish refugee who arrived ten years ago without a penny, borrowed enough to become a peanut vendor, and today runs a prosperous delicatessen and liquor store; an American construction worker who came to Morocco to help build the United States air bases, and has since become a freelance journalist; a Moslem who spent two years in a Spanish jail for voicing his opinions on Generalissimo Franco, and now is a clerk in the municipal administration offices; a tailor from Rome who has not amassed the fortune he had counted on and wants to go home; an English masseuse who was passing through Tangier twenty years ago on a holiday trip and somehow has never left; a Belgian architect who also runs the principal bookshop; a Moslem who taught in the University of Prague for seventeen years and now gives private Arabic lessons; a Swiss businessman who likes the climate and has started a restaurant and bar for his own amusement; an Indian prince who does accounting for an American firm; the Portuguese

Chechaouen—Berber women in the market

seamstress who makes your shirts; and in addition you will be hailed by a good many Spaniards, most of whom were born in Tangier and have never lived anywhere else. The Moslems account for roughly 70 per cent of the population; they still sit in their tiny cafés, drinking tea and coffee, playing cards, checkers and dominoes, shouting above the din of Egyptian music on the radio. Nothing has really changed here either.

Although the people who love Tangier sometimes feel as though there were a conspiracy afoot to make it the most hideous place on earth, actually such a project would prove extremely difficult. With the exception of a few corners of the medina, where the old Moorish architecture has not yet been improved upon, there is nothing left to spoil. And even when the veil has been removed from the face of the last woman to wear one, so she can do her shopping sporting a rayon-satin evening gown four sizes too large for her, and the final old house with a fortresslike façade and one great studded door is demolished to make room for a six-family concrete dwelling with fluorescent lighting in every room, the town will still look very much the same.

With everything old being systematically destroyed (and the new European buildings are almost without exception eyesores, while the ones the Moroccans put up are even worse), how is it that Tangier escapes becoming an aesthetic nightmare? Its topography, more than anything else, I think, saves it; the city is built along the crests and down the flanks of a series of small hills that stand between the sea on one side and a low slightly undulating plain on the other, with high mountains beyond. There are few level stretches in town; at the end of each street there is almost always a natural view, so that the eye automatically skims over that which is near at hand to dwell on a vignette of harbor with ships, or mountain ranges, or sea with distant coastline. Then, the intensity of the sky, even when cloudy, is such that the lighting of these vistas is dramatic, often breathtaking, so that wherever one happens to be, the buildings serve only as an unnoticed frame for the natural beauty beyond. You don't look *at* the city; you look out of it.

The back streets of the medina, crooked, sometimes leading through short tunnels beneath the houses, sometimes up long flights of stairs, lend themselves to solitary speculative walks. With nothing more dangerous than pedestrians and an occasional burro to worry about bumping into, you can devote part of your mind to coming to grips with your ideas. Since I returned here in 1947 I have spent a good many hours wandering through these passageways (incidentally learning to distinguish the thoroughfares from the impasses), busily trying to determine the relationship between Tangier and myself. If you don't know why you like a thing, it is usually worth your while to attempt to find out.

I have not discovered very much, but at least I am now convinced that Tangier is a place where the past and the present exist simultaneously in proportionate degree, where a very much alive today is given an added depth of reality by the presence of an equally alive yesterday. In Europe, it seems to me, the past is largely fictitious; to be aware of it one must have previous knowledge of it. In Tangier the past is a physical reality as perceptible as the sunlight.

Tangier is little more than an enormous market. Since the war it has been primarily a free-money market; and the new autonomous Moroccan government will probably take an increasingly active part in the economic life of a city without currency control. During the international years the dramatic, extralegal facets of the city's character were much publicized, and Tangier was thought of as a place where every fourth person was a smuggler, a spy or a refugee from justice in his native land. It is true that the city was a market where diplomatic information was bought and sold; it was also a place where goods destined to pass eventually across frontiers without benefit of customs inspection were unloaded and reloaded, and, more importantly, a place where people from a variety of nations were able to exist without valid documents to identify them. Then, too, in the absence of all taxes, it was expedient for European exporters to maintain offices here, even though their produce might never pass within a thousand miles of the Moroccan coast. That era is over; such unregulated freedom could hardly continue indefinitely. The withdrawal of foreign business has produced a slump, and there is an

unhealthy amount of unemployment. The shops are stocked with a superfluity of assorted goods from everywhere, and there are not many buyers. The city has no industry—only shopkeepers, agents, hawkers and touts.

Advertisements for watches are everpresent. They flash on and off in the shop windows and flare in neon above the sidewalks. There is an enormous watch sign on a roof at the lower end of the Zoco Chico, in the heart of the medina's principal thoroughfare, made entirely of large sequins, ceaselessly fluttering and glittering above the crowd. All this in a place where for the great majority the smallest unit of time measurement is the *qsim*, which is equal to five of our minutes! But Tangier is very time conscious these days; the youngest children often stop you to inquire gravely what time it is, and listen with obvious relish to your mysterious answer.

Another inescapable feature of the streets is the ubiquitous *cambio*, with its slate bearing the buying and selling rates, in pesetas, of all the world's principal currencies, including the gold dollar. The rates are scribbled in chalk and are subject to change at any moment. The less elaborate *cambios* consist of a chair and a box placed on the sidewalk; the upper end of the Calle Siaghines is lined on both sides with these primitive offices. Personally I have always found that I save money by using a bank.

People here have a fondness for describing Tangier as "central," by which they mean that it is two and a half hours from Gibraltar by ferry, five hours from London by plane, seven hours from Casablanca by car (if you're a careful driver), three days from the beginning of the Sahara Desert by train (assuming there is no sabotage on the line during your journey), and six days from New York by ship. Although the inhabitants of northern Europe consider it a winter resort, those who live here, no doubt having been spoiled by its excellent climate during the rest of the year, often try to escape at that time, because of the torrential rains that come blowing in, usually from the Atlantic. It is not cold, but it is decidedly wet, and if you can find sun by going a few hundred miles southward, it seems foolish not to go. The heavy rains can come at any time from December to April; while you *may* have many weeks of crystalline skies in the course of that period, you can be sure of getting the rains sooner or later, just as you can count on fine weather from the beginning of July onward into November. I often wonder what the climate was like here twenty-five centuries ago, when the place was a trading post called Tingis, run by the Carthaginians from up the coast, and Morocco was a region of dense forests where herds of elephants wandered. I wonder specifically whether the winters could have been any wetter than they are now; I suppose the answer is that they were, but it's difficult to believe.

The basic character of Tangier actually has changed less definitively than its climate. From the beginnings of its known history it has always been in touch with the outside world; its affairs have been administered either directly by representatives of foreign powers or by Moroccans acting in the interests of such powers. For a long time after the fall of Carthage it was a Roman colony; then it was occupied successively by the Vandals, the Byzantines, the Visigoths, the Arabs (who fought over it almost constantly among themselves and with the Islamized Moroccans for eight long centuries), the Portuguese, the Spanish, the Moroccans themselves, eventually with French guidance, and finally the powers represented by the International Commission, of which the three favored members were France, England and Spain. (During World War II Franco, betting on an Axis victory, grabbed it, but was forced to relinquish it to the International Commission at the war's end.) At the moment it is governed by the King of Morocco and militarily occupied by troops of the Moroccan Army.

For years I have been "showing" visitors Tangier. Being an amateur guide in a town that has so many professional ones has its disadvantages, even conceivably its hazards, and in itself is not a particularly enjoyable pastime. But for the nine sight-seers who are mildly amused by the chaos and absurdity of the place, frankly repelled by its ugliness and squalor, or simply indifferent to whatever it may have to offer, there is a tenth one who straightway falls

Tangier—courtyard of the Royal Palace

19

in love with it, and that is the one, of course, who makes the tedious game worthwhile. For this one, as for me, a blank wall at the end of a blind alley suggests mystery, just as being in the tiny closet-like rooms of a Moslem house in the medina evokes the magic of early childhood games, or as the sudden call to prayer of the muezzin from his minaret is a song whose music completely transforms the moment. Such reactions, I have been told, are those of a person who refuses to grow up. If that is so, it is all right with me, to whom being childlike implies having retained the full use of the imagination. For imagination is essential for the enjoyment of a place like Tangier, where the details that meet the eye are not what they seem, but so many points of reference for a whole secret system of overlapping but wildly divergent worlds in the complex life of the city.

What do I show these visitors? Not very much, I'm afraid. Aside from the so-called Sultan's Palace, an eighteenth century construction which now houses a small museum, there are no "points of interest" or historic monuments. In my capacity of cicerone, I have never taken anyone to the Sultan's Palace, because it is not very interesting; it is almost impossible for the visitor to escape it in any case, since every child in the Casbah has one fixed purpose in life, to guide the steps of as many tourists as possible to its entrance door.

Sometimes visitors have wanted to see what they quaintly imagined was called "the red-light district," which consisted of a few back streets on either side of the Zoco Chico. I always let the guides take care of that; anyway, the excursions were invariably unsuccessful, the visitors being bitterly disappointed to find that the Moslem establishments were strictly closed to all but those of the Faith. I use the past tense because, since the coming of independence to Morocco, all brothels have been closed, no matter what the faith of their inmates or prospective clients.

I show visitors the Zoco Chico, whose European-style cafés close these days shortly after midnight. The era is gone when they were open all night, and you could stop by at five in the morning for coffee and watch the tired *tanguistas* from the night clubs being escorted homeward by their pomaded *chulos*. Now the Zoco Chico is a serious and early affair where the customers, mostly Moslems, sit discussing politics over soft drinks and watch, or take part in, the frequent fights that occur in the middle of the square—struggles which break out between the police and unofficial political neighborhood constables, generally over the question of who is to have custody of stray Moslems suspected of having drunk alcohol. Although it is rumored that spirits will be eventually prohibited in this part of the city, there are still plenty of *bodegas* and bars open for business; and as far as the Moslems are concerned, it is safer for them if they simply pretend these establishments don't exist.

The Zoco Chico used to be completely surrounded by sidewalk cafés; slowly these are giving way to curio shops run by members of the ever-increasing colony of Indian merchants, so that now the little square has only five left. Non-Spanish Europeans and Americans patronize the Café Central, probably because it is the largest and brightest. It is also the most consistently besieged by shoeshine boys, beggars, lottery-ticket sellers and wisecracking Moroccan youths trying to force you to buy toothbrushes, toys, fountain pens, fans, razor blades and rayon scarves; so that if you want a quiet conversation, or a half hour with your newspaper over a cup of coffee, it is better to go elsewhere.

Over the years, I have seen the most unlikely people sitting among the *djellabas* and fezzes at the Café Central, from Barbara Hutton to Somerset Maugham and Truman Capote and Cecil Beaton. The other day when I walked past, Errol Flynn was there trying to hide his face behind the pages of a newspaper while a group of Spanish girls stared from what they considered a respectful distance of three feet. Miss Hutton's presence in the Zoco Chico is accounted for by the fact that she is a sometime resident of Tangier, her house being in the medina just around the corner from my own. An important difference between our respective dwellings should be pointed out, however. Hers, I am told, consisted originally of twenty-eight separate Moslem houses which were pulled apart and put together again to make the present structure; mine is still what it always was: a very small and uncomfortable shoe box stood on end.

Tangier—street bazaar

The true center of Tangier is the Zoco de Fuera, an open-air market where the Moslems sell everything from parakeets to buttermilk, from Berber blankets to hot roasted chestnuts, from sofa cushions to Japanese dolls. Eighty years ago the traveler who arrived in Tangier after sunset spent the night here at the foot of the city walls, waiting for the gates to be opened the next morning at dawn. Today the Zoco is a very large square just outside the southern ramparts of the medina—by day a sea of buses, taxis, milling pedestrians and vociferous peddlers. In the middle of this sea is an island which, over the quarter of a century during which I have known it, has grown consistently smaller and less shady as piece after piece of it has been sacrificed to make room for the increasing motor traffic. Storytellers, musicians, acrobats and assorted entertainers used to hold forth here under the trees; in recent years there has grown up a miniature village of rickety little wooden structures with narrow passageways between them. If you don't mind being caught in the crush of Moslems from the country, you can squeeze in and wander through, watching them bargain for big disks of bread and pats of goat cheese. The two wider streets of this island are given over to the display of flowers, incense and cosmetic ingredients such as lumps of alum, henna leaves, shampooing clay and sulfide of antimony for eye make-up.

There is never a moment of the day when the square and the arteries leading into it are not jammed with thousands of voluble vendors and their prospective customers. Late at night, however, a lone voice will echo across its empty darkness, and you can hear, coming from the little wooden stalls, the snores of the watchmen or of the proprietors themselves as they sleep curled up on top of their wares. Before daybreak the long caravans of Berbers and their donkeys which have been moving on their way all night along the country roads toward the city will have arrived, and the goods, mainly foodstuffs, will have been unpacked in one of the big courtyards near the Zoco. The sun will rise on the same scene on which it set the evening before; if it is a Thursday or Sunday there will be even more people from the hills roundabout, for those two days are specifically market days.

The old European residents of the town love the Zoco passionately, and have in the past fought successfully against all plans for modernizing it, cleaning it up, or making a parking lot or a public park out of it. Now that the Moroccans have the power to decide what is to become of it, it is anyone's guess how long it will last, this lively oasis of the past in the midst of today's dreariness. I suspect that it will not disappear before the people who run it are willing to have it go, and since fortunately they are not too interested in change for change's sake—unlike the city Moslems, who have been infected with the progress virus—the din, smoke and brilliant confusion of the Zoco may remain in our midst a little longer.

(I underestimated the zeal of civic-minded Moroccans. Almost as soon as this was written the market was pulled down; gravel walks were laid and flowers planted in its stead. A few hundred feet from the old site, however, behind the Mosque of Sidi Bouabid, space is being cleared for a new Zoco de Fuera, and sometime in 1958 we shall have our new market.)

Usually I take my wards to see the beaches and the Mountain. For those who prefer company while they bathe there is the municipal beach, a fine five-mile semicircle of sand bordering the Bay of Tangier, and within walking distance of all the hotels; for lovers of solitude there is the vast Atlantic beach stretching southward from the Grottoes of Hercules in a straight white band as far as the eye can see, across the Oued Tahadartz and on into what used to be the Spanish Zone. This is utterly unspoiled and one of the most beautiful beaches I know. The Mountain, the highest point of which is about a thousand feet above the port, is heavily forested with eucalyptus, parasol pine and cypress, and is considered the pleasantest place in all Tangier to live. Three hundred years ago these forest lands served as a base of operations for the Moroccans in their successful war to liberate Tangier from the British. Today, however, the British have got a good part of them back again, for it is largely they who own and live on the Mountain. There are also the palaces of two defunct sultans: the palace of Ben Arafa, who was not a sultan but had to play the part of one when the French exiled the present monarch in

1953; and the romantically isolated Villa Perdicaris, looking like something out of Sir Walter Scott, which was bought by the Pasha el Glaoui not long before that unpopular notable's death in 1956.

During the summer of 1957 it was announced officially that His Highness Mohammed V intends to make Tangier his summer capital. Whether this will actually happen remains to be seen, but many people here, convinced that this would provide a solution to the local economic crisis, are holding their breath in hope that the rumor will turn out to be true. My own suspicion is that the soaring prices which would result would mean the end of Tangier as one of the cheapest places for an American to live in, whatever miracles it might perform for the town's economy.

When the visitor has seen the Zocos and beaches and palaces, he still has not seen the city's most important single phenomenon, the one which gives reality to and determines the ultimate meaning of all the others: I mean the spectacle of the average Moroccan's daily life. This necessitates going into the homes, preferably those of the lower middle class, and into the small neighborhood cafés which have a strictly Moslem clientele.

The cafés are not as accessible as they used to be, since the recent upsurge of nationalist feeling has somewhat modified the attitude of amicable indifference which the Moslem used to show toward the anonymous foreigner. For this reason it is important for me to choose places where my face is known, where I can still get a jovial greeting from the proprietor and thus be assured a reasonably friendly reception on the part of the patrons.

In the back of practically every such establishment there is an open space covered with reed matting, generally raised above the level of the floor; entry into this part of the room demands the removal of one's shoes.

Here the men sit with their legs tucked under them and, more often than not, in spite of the unofficial prohibition, pull out their kif pipes and smoke them as they always have done. The cafés are like men's clubs. A man frequents the same one year in and year out. Often he brings his food and eats there; sometimes he stretches out on the matting and sleeps there. His café is his mail address, and rather than use his home, where there are always womenfolk about, he will use the café for keeping his social appointments. In the smaller cafés, the entrance of anyone from outside the familiar circle of daily habitués has always been regarded with a wary eye and a certain degree of suspicion. Each café has its own little legends and references which can be understood only by the initiates. It is here that the endless stories and complicated jokes which so delight the Moslem mind are told, and where the average man is at his happiest and least inhibited.

If a café happens to offer any kind of native Moroccan music, which is extremely rare these days, I will force my way through any wall of hostile stares in order to get a seat and listen; I suppose not many visitors are that eager to hear Moroccan café music.

The casual outsider, however, can usually get more glimpses of café life than he can of home life. In a bourgeois household, upon the entry of any man or boy not of the immediate family, Moslem or otherwise, all the women and girls are swiftly hidden, and remain hidden until he goes out of the house. In families of lower income, on the other hand, the social strictures have been considerably relaxed, so that I have only to suggest to my maid or chauffeur that a group of my friends would like to visit a Moslem home and meet all the members of the family, and the invitation will be willingly extended. I don't claim that the activities which we see in a Moslem home are identical with those which would be going on if we were not there. But if we stay long enough, a certain degree of relaxation is usually reached, and the household rhythm at length begins to pulse of its own accord, so that it is possible to get a pretty clear picture of what life is like in the domestic citadel.

By our standards these people are desperately poor. At present, for instance, the maid who gets our breakfast, cleans the five rooms, and does all the laundering of our clothes, earns the equivalent of $8.33 a month. Also, she gets no food from us. Even in Tangier that is a low wage for 1958. Yet if

Chechaouen—the tower of the Casbah

27

Chechaouen—street scene

Chechaouen—street scene

you visit her house, you find it immaculate; moreover, the manner of life that she and her family lead manages to give an impression of Oriental ease and even abundance. It is a peculiarly Moslem gift, being able to create the illusion of luxury in the midst of poverty, and it never fails to arouse my admiration when I see it displayed. But then, these people are the supreme illusionists; they can give a straightforward action the air of being a conjurer's trick or make the most tortuously devious behavior seem like naturalness itself.

I have never decided precisely why the time spent in these humble homes is so satifying. Perhaps it is merely because both hosts and guests are playing a simple, pleasant game in which the hosts lead the way with regard to the silences to be observed as well as the conversation to be made, and the guests follow comfortably, happy to have all social responsibility taken from them. Certainly it is agreeable now and then to spend an evening reclining peaceably among piles of cushions, in effortless talk with people who are completely natural but infinitely polite. And when the end of the evening comes, and they have fully convinced you that the occasion has been even more enjoyable for them than for you, and you have pronounced the necessary formulas of farewell, it is delightful too, to step out into the silent moonlit street, and a moment later look from a Casbah gateway down upon the thousands of white cubes which are the houses of the medina, hearing only the waves as they break on the beach and perhaps the sleepy antiphonal crowing of two roosters on neighboring rooftops. If I ask myself occasionally whether I may not be a trifle out of my mind to have chosen to spend so many years in this crazy city, it is at such moments that I am reassured—easily able to convince myself that if it were 1931 once more, and I possessed the gift of accurately foretelling the future, I should very likely take Miss Stein's good advice and make my first journey to Tangier all over again.

FEZ: BEHIND THE WALLS

If you came down out of the mountains from Ouezzane, you saw it far below—a whitish-gray spot ringed with green. From that distance, it was unrecognizable as a city; it might have been a quarry or a simple discoloration in the plain. As you swung around the curves on your way down the flank of Djebel Zalagh, the spot broadened constantly, and a definite line separating the gray part from the green became visible: It was the wall surrounding the medina, the old city center. Within were tens of thousands of cube-shaped structures, their pattern varied here and there by the thin prism of a minaret reaching above them. Outside the line were the fruit orchards and olive groves that brought the country to the very foot of the wall, enclosing the city in a solid frame of verdure, so that from this vantage point it was like a white bouquet tightly encased in leaves. In the past two decades, the city has burst through its confines at several points and grown new additions outside the ramparts. But from above it looks much the same.

To call Fez one of the great cities of the world might seem to some a generous gesture. It is not commercially or industrially important; it is no longer a cultural or political center; it does not even have the most impressive examples of its own architectural style (which are not to be found in Morocco at all, but in Spain). Unlike other cities that enjoyed their period of greatness in remote times, and that are judged worthy of more or less attention according to the number of historical vestiges they contain, Fez does not have to rely upon its ancient structures for its claim to importance. Its interest lies not so much in relics of the past as in the life of the people there; that life *is* the past, still alive and functioning. It would be difficult to find another city anywhere in which the everyday vicissitudes of medieval urban life can be studied in such detail. Here is a city of more than half a million people who spend their time at such occupations as hammering and chasing brass and copper, tanning and tooling leather, carding, spinning, and weaving wool, and all the other slow processes whereby the raw materials of the land are transformed into artifacts. (These objects, originally designed for the Moroccan market, are now made with the tourist trade in mind, and there is a corresponding deterioration of their workmanship.)

The visitor senses something in Fez that he describes as a feeling of mystery; that is as good a way as any of describing the impression the city makes. There is no doubt that to the person with a little imagination that impression is very strong. The city seems inexhaustible, incredibly complex, and vaguely menacing. It is possible that the visitor will also find it beautiful, although this is by no means certain. Fez is not a city that everyone can like. Many travelers have a negative reaction to its dark twisting alleys, teeming with people and animals. Anyone subject to claustrophobia may well find it only a nightmarish welter of tunnels, dead-end passageways, and windowless walls. To grasp the fascination of the place one has to be the sort of person who enjoys losing himself in a crowd and being pushed along by it, not caring where to or for how long. He must be able to attain relaxation in the idea of being helpless in the midst of that crowd; he must know how to find pleasure in the outlandish and see beauty where it is most unlikely to appear.

One of the city's chief attractions (for the visitor) is also one of its major annoyances (for the inhabitants): its ancient wall. These miles of walls without which Fez could not have existed, are beginning to stifle the city; in some places, people have done what was formerly unthinkable and have built

Fez—entering the medina

houses outside the ramparts. There are not many gates, and to get out it is necessary often to make long detours. With the passage of time the wall seems destined to be reduced to a few vestiges of itself. New gateways will be cut through from the crowded interior to the open spaces outside. Eventually, whatever is left of the wall will be lost in the new structures made inevitable by the fast-growing population and the unfolding of the city's economy. For the moment, however, the wall provides a precise demarcation between outside and inside. Automobiles can go through certain gates, but nowhere is it possible for them to continue very far. The ingenuous motorist who imagines that because he has got in, he is going to be able to go on, is in for a sad surprise. The street, narrow from the beginning, is suddenly allowing the walls to touch the car on both sides, and he has got to go back where he came from, but in reverse.

There is a good deal of frustration involved in the process of enjoying Fez. The blank wall is its symbol, but it is this very secretiveness that gives the city its quality. The Fassi feels intuitively that everything should be hidden: the practice of his religion, his personal possessions (including his womenfolk), and above all his thoughts. If anyone besides him knows what he really thinks, he is already compromised, at a disadvantage, since his mind functions largely in terms of strategy. (Moroccans in general are not an "Oriental" people, but the bourgeois of Fez are.)

BEYOND CIVILIZATION

I have noticed that the inhabitants have a minimal interest in what exists immediately outside the limits of their city. The dozen miles or so of high ramparts have consistently shut out not only the Berber's unwelcome person, but also his incompatible African culture. Some years ago, I was working on a project for the Rockefeller Foundation, recording folk and art music throughout the country. This had to be done in collaboration with the Moroccan government. Inevitably, I came to Fez and presented my credentials to the *katib* of the governor. "Folk music!" he snorted. "I detest folk music! It is precisely this sort of thing that we are doing our best to stamp out."

Nevertheless, since he was a Moroccan and I was a foreigner in his country, he also felt it incumbent upon him to give me some sort of assistance, so eventually I found myself talking with a group of young musicians who played *chaabiya*, or popular urban music. One of them politely asked me in which city I had so far made most of my recordings. I said that the great majority of them had been made not in any city, but in the country. My answer seemed to bewilder him. "In the country? But there is no music in the country."

I said that my experience had been that there was music practically everywhere in Morocco. He smiled. "Oh, you mean the Berbers! I've never heard any of their music."

"Surely you must have," I said. "You can hear it only a short distance from here, up that way, down that way"—I pointed—"around Tahala or Rhafaii, for instance."

He smiled again, this time at my ignorance. "Nobody ever goes to such places," he said categorically. Aware of that, I still feigned innocence. "Why not?" I demanded. I was told: "Because there's nothing there. The people are like savages."

The Fassi is a metropolitan, bourgeois in his habits and isolationist in his attitude; he also has the reputation of being a hard man to beat in a business deal, making him not entirely popular with his compatriots. There is no doubt that he has an element of arrogance in his character. Aware that his city was a cultural hub of all North Africa, he has been content to let others come to him in order to learn. Civilization ended at the gates of the medina; outside was the wilderness.

Fez—a trellised street in the medina

From the earliest days, the growth of the city has followed a particular pattern that might have been expected to destroy it rather than to play a part in its development. The place seems to carry the element of dissension within its very foundations. It has been a schizophrenic city from the outset, since, early in the ninth century, the two communities that formed its original nucleus were founded. Each time its two parts have been unified, a rival town has sprung into existence next door, an entity that in its turn had to be subdued and ultimately amalgamated. And, from without, the place has been besieged, flooded, pillaged, burned, and bombarded so often that it seems incredible there should be anything at all left of it, much less the architecturally homogeneous mass that it is. Through the centuries, the reigning dynasties have been obliged to wage war against the inhabitants in order to make them recognize their sovereignty. Being prepared for a siege is so much a part of the pattern of life that some middle- and upper-class citizens are inclined to keep a large supply of staple foods in their houses, "just in case."

The conditions responsible for this display of mass anxiety have not changed basically in the eleven hundred years since the founding of the city. One could use Fez as an object lesson to illustrate the play of forces in the city-versus-country struggle that operates throughout Morocco and determines much of its character. Fez was built at a natural crossroads, the spot where the route from the Sahara to the Mediterranean coast intersects the east-west passage between Algeria and the Atlantic. To impose an economic stranglehold on the newly conquered land it was imperative that the Arabs control these principal arteries of transit. Automatically, Fez became the strategic center, the command of which was a sine qua non for the administration of the entire region. Within the walls there grew up a prosperous commercial city with an imported Semitic culture, while directly outside in the surrounding hills, in full view of the town, lived the infinitely less evolved Berbers, upon whose precarious goodwill the urban dwellers' peace of mind largely depended. The pagan Berbers accepted the new monotheistic religion of Islam, but clashes between two such dissimilar groups were inevitable. Despite the government's efforts to create a more homogeneous population, the friction still persists.

THE HEART OF THE CITY

The street goes down and down, always unpaved, nearly always partially hidden from the sky. Sometimes, it is so narrow as to permit only one-way foot traffic; here the beasts of burden scrape their flanks on each side as they squeeze through, and you have to back up or step quickly into a doorway while they pass, the drivers intoning, "*Balak, balak, balak.*" Here is the bitter earth odor of new pottery, here the rank smell of hides being tanned, or the stench of a butcher's stall where the meat, black with flies, ripens in the shaft of dusty sunlight that points like an accusing finger down through the meshes of the latticework. In dark recesses like grottoes are mosaic fountains where women and girls scream invectives as they fill their pails and the dust under their feet turns to mud. Then you are walking under an elaborately carved portal hung with ancient bronze lanterns, and you smell the feline scent of fig trees. A cascade of water rumbles nearby, but it is behind a wall and you never catch a glimpse of it.

Even in the heart of the city a surprising amount of space is devoted to private gardens. As he follows the winding, shut-in streets, the passerby cannot divine the presence of the pleasure spots behind the high walls. But they are there, and for those who are lucky enough to possess them, they add immeasurably to the charm of living in Fez.

From the street, a house is a high wall with a door somewhere along its uneven length and possibly a handful of tiny grilled peepholes sprinkled in a haphazard design across its surface. Some 30 feet above the ground there may be a huge cedar beam sprouting from the façade at a 45-degree angle and supporting a triangular bay that juts out high above the street, providing the raison d'être for that vast expanse of virtually empty wall below it. With

Fez—a view of the city from the ruins of Borj Sud (South Fort)

the exception of the door, which is usually studded in a mosaic of brass nail heads, there is no suggestion of decoration or even of a preoccupation with the kind of surface given to the adobe or plaster that covers the wall.

The inside of the house is another matter. When you step into the glittering tile and marble interior of a prosperous Fez dwelling, with its orange trees and its fountains and the combined pastel and hard-candy colors glowing from the rooms around the courtyard, you are pleased that there should be nothing but the indifferent anonymity of a blank wall outside—nothing to indicate the existence of this very private, remote, and brilliant world within.

In the less sumptuous homes, the door necessarily opens directly upon the patio. Nevertheless, even here from the street nothing is visible but a short blind corridor that makes a right-angle turn before opening into the courtyard. This is invariable. Whether the women are visible or hidden, their presence and collective personality are constantly suggested by the diaphanous curtains of white muslin that hang across the doorways and around the canopied beds; it is impossible to imagine the color schemes in the rooms, either, save in relation to the women who live in them. The men are in and out of the house, day and night—no one can be expected to know where a man may be—but the women pass their lives inside the house, and this is evident.

Right: Fez—in the tannery

Following pages: Fez—leather dyeing vats in the tannery

A courtyard may have as many as three galleries that go part or all the way around it; the rooms can be reached only by going along the galleries. Stairways are steep, inlaid with mosaics of very small tiles, and sometimes tipped with white marble treads. The house looks in upon itself; the focus of attention is a stone basin of water in the center. The women must have total protection from the world without. The architect, having provided this, is then free to become decorator and can concentrate his attention upon the delights of applied geometric design in plaster filigree, carved wood, and paint. A large house may have several separate patios, each one multiple-storied and with many rooms; a humble house has a central open space with two or three rooms giving onto it. The very poor sometimes live in rooming houses, each family occupying one room and having the use of that section of the gallery outside the door, conditions which necessarily give rise to disputes about rights to space and violation of private property.

Fez is still a relatively relaxed city; there is time for everything. The retention of this classic sense of time can be attributed, in part at least, to the absence of motor vehicles in the medina. If you live in a city where you never have to run in order to catch something, or jump to avoid being hit by it, you are likely to have preserved a natural physical dignity that is not a concomitant of contemporary life.

For all their religious orthodoxy and outward austerity, the people of Fez are not ashamed to be hedonists. They love the sound of a fountain

splashing in the courtyard; on the coals of their braziers they sprinkle sandalwood and benzoin; they have a passion for sitting on a high spot of ground at twilight and watching the slow change of light, color, and form in the landscape. Outside the ramparts are innumerable orchards, delightful little wildernesses of canebrake, where olive and fig trees abound. It is the custom for families to go out there on a late afternoon with their rugs, braziers, and tea equipment. One discovers groups of such picnickers in the most secluded corners of the countryside, particularly on the northern slopes above the valley. Not long ago on one of my walks I came upon a family spread out in the long grass. They were sitting quietly on their reed mats, but something in their collective attitude made me stop and observe them more closely. Then I saw that surrounding them at a radius of perhaps 100 feet was a circle of bird cages, each supported by a stake driven into the ground. There were birds in all the cages, and they were singing. The entire family sat there happily, listening. As urbanites in other places carry along their radios, they had brought their birds with them, purely for entertainment.

The changes brought about during the 54 years since I first saw Fez are relatively superficial; none has been so drastic as to alter its image. The medina is protected by the form of the land on which it was built; its topography is roughly funnel-shaped, and it is not likely to be bulldozed like so much of Cairo in the time of Abdel Nasser. Yet with the increasing poverty in the region the city clearly cannot continue much longer in its present form. Those of the original inhabitants who can afford it are moving to Casablanca, leaving the medina at the mercy of the impoverished rustics replacing them. A house that formerly sheltered one family now contains 10 or 12 families, living, it goes without saying, in unimaginable squalor. The ancient dwellings are falling rapidly into disrepair. And so at last, it is the people from outside the walls who have taken over the city, and their conquest, a natural and inevitable process, spells its doom. That Fez should still be there today, unchanged in its outward form, is the surprising phenomenon.

Right: Fez—looking into the interior of the Karaouine Mosque

Following pages: Left: Fez—the interior of the Zaouia Mosque of Moulay Idris, seen through a carved wooden portal

Right: Meknès—interior of the tomb of Moulay Ismael

Above: Meknès—ruins of the old Royal Stable

Following pages: Meknès—fields of sunflowers

47

A Café in Morocco

The beach, very wide along this coast, is protected by a crumbling breakwater a few hundred feet offshore, so that from here in the garden the waves make only a distant murmur, a somnolent backdrop for the nearer sounds of bees buzzing and the occasional low voices of the men inside the café. I came into the garden a few minutes ago and sat down on a large woven-grass mat near the well. The mat has been provided with piles of bottle tops to be used as counters in whatever game I may be going to play.

The garden spreads out along the foot of the town's ramparts, hidden behind a jungle of fig trees and cactus, buried in total shade beneath a ceiling of grape leaves. At this season the heavy bunches of grapes hang down between the meshes of cane trellis above, and bump against my forehead as I come through on my way to the well. Facing me, in a corner, like a Chinese lantern big enough to hold a man, is a wicker fish trap left to dry: this is a fishermen's café. At night, after it is shut and the beach is deserted, the customers often return with their own teapots and invade the garden, lying on the mats talking and smoking, and when the grapes and figs are ripe, eating the fruit. Mrhait, who runs the establishment, finds this as it should be. "The fruit is here for our friends to eat," he declares. There are a few tables and chairs around for those who want them, and even these are left out all night for the customers' convenience. They represent the major part of his capital, and they could easily be carried away. But this is a small town; no one has ever stolen anything from him.

The traditional café in this part of the world is conceived of as a club where, in addition to enjoying the usual amenities of a café, a man may, if he wishes, eat, sleep, bathe and store his personal effects. The fact that the nearest café may be five or ten minutes' walk from where he lives (it is seldom farther, for the establishments are numerous) does not prevent him from considering it an extension of his home. Each café has its regular clientele whose members know one another; the habitués form a limited little community in which the appearance of an unfamiliar local face is as much an intrusion as that of a complete foreigner. It is difficult to induce a Muslim to go into a café where he is not known: he does not enjoy being stared at.

Upper-class Muslims generally refuse to be seen in cafés at all, their contention being that one sits and drinks tea in a crowded public place only if one cannot do so in one's own house. But for these good bourgeois, as for us Europeans, the taking of tea is thought of as a relaxing pause, a respite from the affairs of the day. The hour or two spent on the terrace of a café counts as time off from the involvements of daily routine; one sits and watches life go past. The average Muslim here, on the contrary, goes into a café in order to participate as intensely as possible in the collective existence of his friends and neighbors. In a land whose social life is predicated on the separation of the sexes, the home is indisputably the woman's precinct; the man must seek his life outside. And the generally prevalent uproar in even the middle-class Muslim household makes the all-male café a necessity. Only there does the man feel free to talk, smoke his kif pipe, play or listen to music, and even, if the spirit moves him, to dance a little in front of his friends.

And it is in the café that the foreign visitor, too, can feel the pulse of the country. Nowhere else can he manage to observe a group of individuals repeatedly and at length in their daily contacts with one another, or succeed in existing at their tempo, achieving in occasional unguarded moments a state of empathy with their very different sense of the passage of time. And to experience time from the vantage point of these people is essential to understanding their attitudes and behavior. Today, when even in the farthest reaches of the bush there is beginning to be established a relationship

Above: Rabat—the streets of the Casbah

Following pages: Rabat—a view of the Casbah, largely built by descendants of the Moors forced to flee Spain after 1492

between the number of hours a man works and the amount of wages he collects, any human institution where the awareness of time has not yet penetrated is a phenomenon to be cherished.

With its luxury of unmeasured time the Moroccan café is out of harmony with present-day concepts, and thus it is doomed to extinction. Ask any café owner. It takes approximately three minutes to prepare each glass of tea. The customer may then sit for as many hours as he wishes over one glass. Since the maximum profit per order is equivalent to about one cent, it seems clear that economically there is no future in the café business. There are other factors, too, that militate against the continued life of the traditional "Moorish" café. It is claimed by the authorities that cafés cause men to waste time that might be used to better advantage. Whatever places are shut down in periods of civic reform (and latter-day puritanism has made these campaigns fairly frequent) are thereby permanently destroyed, since if and when they are reopened, it is invariably as European-style establishments. The change-over in clothing also has its effect. As long as the clientele was composed exclusively of men wearing the customary garments, it was sufficient to cover the floor with grass matting. The increasing number of those who sport European apparel, however, induces the owners to provide chairs, since the Moroccans like their trousers to be so tight-fitting that to sit in their normal position on the floor while wearing them would be an impossibility.

The traditional floor-café is a result of natural processes; one might say it is strictly functional, in that the intent is merely to make as comfortable and pleasant a place as possible for the greatest number of people, and at minimum cost. The cheapest materials—cane, bamboo, palm thatch, woven reeds and grass—are not only the most attractive visually, but also provide the most satisfactory acoustics for the music. The modern table-and-chair café, on the other hand, is an abstraction: its primary aim has come to be the showing off of the expensive foreign objects that have been acquired (including, in the cities, electric refrigerator and television) and that distinguish the place from its humbler rivals. Practical considerations fade before the determination to make this all-important display. Thus it is that the new-style cafés achieve only a sordid uniformity in their discomfort and metallic noisiness, while the old-fashioned places are as diverse as the individuals who created them.

This garden here by the sea with its ceiling of grapes; the flat roofs of the Marrakesh cafés where men sit at midnight waiting for a breath of cool air; the cavelike rooms in the mountain markets of the High Atlas, to which the customers must bring their own tea, sugar and mint, the establishment furnishing only the fire, water and teapot; in Fez the baroque wooden palaces among the weeping willows of the Djenane es Sebir, whose deck chairs line the river's wandering channels; the cafés where the tea drinkers bring their prayer mats and retire into a small carpeted room to perform their sundown prostrations; the countless little niches in the alleys of every town, where a plank along the wall and bottle crates turned on end are the only furnishings; and then the cafés with dancing boys, like the Stah in Tangier; the sanctuary cafés, whose shadiest customers remain unmolested by the authorities, like the one opposite the gardens of the Koutoubia in Marrakesh; the superb improvised tent cafés at the great religious pilgrimages in the wilderness; the range is vast. Few countries can supply such a variety of décor and atmosphere.

And what goes on in these places? The men converse, tell interminable stories, eat, smoke kif, sleep, and play games: cards, checkers, dominoes, parchisi and, during Ramadan, bingo, whose prize used to be a glass of tea for each winner, but which nowadays often mysteriously turns out to be a bottle of cooking oil. In cold weather they sit as near as they can to the bed of burning charcoal under the water boiler. At night latecomers anxiously ask as they enter: "Is there still fire?" Once the embers have been allowed to die there is no more tea until the next day. The water boiler is an improvised samovar made of copper with a tap on the side; once in a while it proves to be the real article, with Cyrillic characters incised on its flank. Being the most important item in the place, it is put in the spot where there is the most light.

Ouzoude—a waterfall

Rabat—the interior of the tomb of Mohammed V, father of present King Hassan II

Rabat—the doors of the tomb of Mohammed V

The elaboration of niches and shelves around the fire and water is the living heart of the café—rather like the altar of a church. In the cities it is a complicated tile-covered construction that serves as sink, stove and cabinet. One compartment contains the fire and the samovar, another the water tap or pail; smaller cubicles are for storing sugar, tea and mint. In the lesser cafés the single table is put beside this unlikely looking installation. Close friends of the proprietor and the kif concessionaire generally sit here. Nowadays, what with official frowns being directed at the smoking of the herb, the kif seller is not likely to be in evidence; nevertheless, he is a very important factor in the functioning of the café. He not only brings his own raw material, which traditionally he cleans and cuts in full view of the clients before selling it to them, thus forestalling doubts about its purity, but also processes (for a price) the kif that others have brought with them, blending the tobacco with it to suit each man's individual taste. How much of this must go on clandestinely depends on local circumstances; the ban on kif is being enforced with increasing firmness.

Unless he has been at the pipe for many hours, it is impossible to tell from a North African's behavior whether or not he has smoked kif. The same observation cannot be made, I am afraid, if alcohol has been taken instead. In the bars, loosened inhibitions send tempers up in flames, but I have never seen anything more serious than an argument in a café full of men smoking kif; the prevailing atmosphere is calm and jovial.

When the tea maker gets an order, he takes a long-handled tin canister and puts in a heaping teaspoonful of green China tea (usually Formosan chun mec). Next he adds four or five teaspoonfuls of sugar. Another little canister filled with hot water from the samovar is already embedded in the coals. As soon as it is boiling, he pours the water over the mixed tea and sugar. While it is steeping he crushes as many stalks of fresh spearmint as he can into the glass. Then he strains the tea into the glass, often garnishing it with a sprig of verbena, two or three unopened orange blossoms, or a few leaves of rosemary, *chiba* or some other locally available herb. The result, hot, sweet and strongly aromatic, bears very little resemblance to tea as it is drunk anywhere else in the world; it is *até*, a refresher in its own right, not unlike *maté* in Argentina but a good deal more tasty. Usually when newcomers try their first glass, they are appalled by the concentrated sweetness, and get into the habit of ordering it with less sugar. The results are catastrophic. Indeed, the cafés that cater to the tourist trade now serve an unpalatable hybrid concoction, neither *até* nor tea. The Moroccans were quick to heed the foreigners' preferences: what with the constantly rising cost of sugar, the new preparation saves them money.

All cafés provide neighborhood delivery service. A boy carries racks holding six glasses, back and forth, full and empty, all day long between the samovar and the nearby offices, banks and shops. Boiling-hot mint tea is still the favorite drink in the land, notwithstanding the increasing sales of colas and other bottled gaseous beverages. Even the customs officials in the port may be sipping tea offhandedly while they go through the luggage; the traveler who is automatically unnerved by the prospect of customs inspection often finds this reassuring.

A part of each café is occupied by the *soudda*, a wooden platform raised a foot or so above the floor, usually with a low railing around it, and always with a covering of woven grass or reed matting. If there are any musicians they sit here, as do the establishment's most regular and esteemed habitués. After hours at night, this space may be used as a dormitory for transients. Ten or twelve years ago in the Calle Ben Charki of Tangier there was a large café with an unusual clientele. It made no difference whether you went at midnight or at three in the morning: scores of boys between the ages of eight and fourteen sat at the tables in the center of the sparsely lighted room, fiercely playing cards. A wide platform extended along three of the walls, where there was even less light. The boys lying here tossed and scratched in their sleep; even so, they were the lucky ones, for when the card players began

Above: Rabat—a shrine in The Chellah

Left: Rabat—view of the ruins of The Chellah

to yawn and look around for a place to stretch out, the platform was often full, and they had to be content to move to a table where others were already asleep, leaning forward from the little straight-backed chairs, their heads and arms lying flat on the boards. Month in, month out, the ragged horde filled the café. They were the *boleros* of Tangier, children who had strayed into the city from the hills beyond, and having managed to acquire a wooden box, a tin or two of polish, an old toothbrush and a rag, had set themselves up in business as shoeshine boys. As an old resident, I found the place a natural concomitant of North African life; however, the foreign visitors I took there thought it offensive. Children ought not to live that way. Apparently the authorities shared these prejudices, for the establishment has long since ceased to function, nor are there any others similar to it.

Like all the African countries, Morocco has been thrown open to the forces of rapid modernization. The fact that its indigenous culture is so much more highly evolved than that of most other places on the continent tends, however, to retard the process. In a primitive land where the disparity between the old and the new worlds is total, the conversion conceivably can be effected in one generation, but where there is a perfectly viable, if archaic, tradition of civilization already in existence, as there is in Morocco, it will naturally take more time. This spirit of resistance to arbitrary, senseless change is a stock subject of the humorous anecdotes exchanged among café sitters, particularly in small towns.

A story I heard here in Mrhait's café the other day delighted me. This was a factual account of something that happened in a little country market up in the hills behind Larache. It was the day of the week when all the peasants of the region come on foot and on donkeyback to the village and sit in the market selling the things they have brought in with them. Swaggering through the throng of rustics came a young man who, if he was not really from the city, at least was doing everything he could to create that impression, his most blatant claim to urban refinement being a brand-new pair of locally made Levis, so skin-tight that he had a little difficulty in walking. He came up to an old woman, one among many others like her, who sat in the dust with a few figs, a half dozen green peppers and some tomatoes, each being arranged according to custom in a neat little pyramid in front of her. Indicating the figs with the toe of his shoe, and thus upsetting the pile, the youth asked their price in an offhand manner calculated to widen the social difference he felt existed between him and the old woman.

"Don't kick the fruit, my son," she said evenly. She had taken his measure as he came, but now she did not even look up at him. Then she added: "If you'll sit down here beside me, I'll give you a good price."

The prospect of a bargain proved too much for the young man. He squatted down, and that was the end of him. With an explosive sound the seams of his trousers split wide open. ("His face was red, red!" the raconteur recalled with relish.) To the accompaniment of loud peasant laughter the young man made his way back through the crowd and out of the market.

One night I went to Mrhait's café with the idea of telling him that what I had been writing there at the end of his garden was a piece about cafés, to see if he had anything to say on the subject. But I intended to wait until everyone had gone, in order to avoid interruptions. It was fairly late, and there was a hot east wind roaring overhead. Even there behind the ramparts I recognized the dry spicy smell of parched hillsides that is borne on the *cherqi* at this time of year. The waves rolled in across the dark beach with mechanical regularity. I sat until there was no one in the garden and I could hear no voices inside the café. Eventually Mrhait came out of the doorway and peered through the tangle of vines toward my dim corner. He finally saw me and came over.

After he had sat down opposite me and lighted a cigarette, I began. "You know, I've been writing about cafés here in Morocco so that Americans will know what they're like. I thought maybe you might have something to say about your own café, something you'd like them to know."

Essaouira—a street scene

Essaouira—ramparts of the old fort

The cigarette end flared; his voice betrayed a surprising degree of feeling. "For sixteen years, ever since I was twelve and my father put me in this café, I've worked here and lived here and slept here. I made all this with my own hands. Why are those roses growing there? Because I planted the bushes. Why do we have these figs and grapes? Because I take care of the trees and vines. Why is there good sweet water in the well? Because I keep it clean. This morning, this very day, I went down inside and scooped out eight wheelbarrows full of sand and mud. That's what it means to run a café—not making one glass or a thousand glasses of tea."

Failing to see just where his rhetoric was leading him, I interrupted cautiously: "But you do like your work, don't you?"

"My work is in the garden, and that's only in summer. In the winter I stay inside the café, and the wind blows, and some days nobody comes at all. Just the empty café, and outside the rain and the waves. That's not work. That's prison. There's nobody left in this town. Everybody's gone. And that's why I'm going to go to the city myself and get a job in a café where they pay you every week."

He rose to his feet. I was silent, considering again the transitoriness of everything in this land. In my imagination the café had long ago assumed the character of a landmark; it seemed impossible that Mrhait should be willing to walk out and leave it. I got up, too, and followed him slowly across the garden.

"But it's your café!" I was saying. "It belongs to you! After all these years you want to begin working for wages? At your age?"

In front of the doorway onto the beach he stopped and turned to face me. "Look. If you can't make a living by working for yourself, then you go to work for somebody else, don't you?"

"I suppose so."

"It's better to carry glasses in a busy café than own an empty one. Better to eat than starve, no?"

As we shook hands, he added reassuringly: "I'll be back. I'm sure to come back, later on. Just as soon as I get a little money together."

Fortunately it was dark and he did not see my smile, which he would have recognized as cynical. The familiar refrain: *There is money in the city! I'm going to get it.* Whether or not Mrhait gets it, once he has lived in the city he will not return here.

Above: Moulay Idris—detail of an ironwork doorway

Right: El Jadidah—a sixteenth century cistern, built by the Portuguese

Essaouira—a woman in traditional garb

Above: Essaouira—a street scene

Following pages: El Jadidah—the port and ramparts of the old fort

73

T_{HE} M_{OSLEMS}

It had taken the truck fourteen hours to get from Kerzaz to Adrar, and except for the lunch stop in the oasis of El Aougherout, the old man had sat the whole time on the floor without moving, his legs tucked up beneath him, the hood of his burnoose pulled up over his turban to protect his face from the fine dust that sifted up through the floor. First-class passage on the vehicles of the Compagnie Générale Transsaharienne entitled the voyager to travel in the glassed-in compartment with the driver, and that was where I sat, occasionally turning to look through the smeared panes at the solitary figure sitting sedately in the midst of the tornado of dust behind. At lunchtime, when I had seen his face with its burning brown eyes and magnificent white beard, it had occurred to me that he looked like a handsome and very serious Santa Claus.

The dust grew worse during the afternoon, so that by sunset, when we finally pulled into Adrar, even the driver and I were covered. I got out and shook myself, and the little old man clambered out of the back, cascades of dust spilling from his garments. Then he came around to the front of the truck to speak to the driver, who, being a good Moslem, wanted to get to a shower and wash himself. Unfortunately he was a city Moslem as well, so that he was impatient with the measured cadence of his countryman's speech, and slammed the door in the middle of it, unaware that the old man's hand was in the way.

Calmly the old man opened the door with his other hand. The tip of his middle finger dangled by a bit of skin. He looked at it an instant, then quietly scooped up a handful of that ubiquitous dust, put the two parts of the finger together and poured the dust over it, saying softly: "Thanks be to Allah." With that, the expression on his face never having changed, he picked up his bundle and staff and walked away. I stood looking after him, full of wonder, and reflecting upon the differences between his behavior and what mine would have been under the same circumstances. To show no outward sign of pain is unusual enough, but to express no resentment against the person who has hurt you seems very strange, and to give thanks to God at such a moment is the strangest touch of all.

My experience since then has shown me that this was not untypical, and it has remained in my memory and become a symbol of that which is admirable in the people of North Africa. "This world we see is unimportant and ephemeral as a dream," they say. "To take it seriously would be an absurdity. Let us think rather of the heavens that surround us." And the landscape is conducive to reflections upon the nature of the infinite. In other parts of Africa you are aware of the earth beneath your feet, of the vegetation and the animals; all power seems concentrated in the earth. In North Africa the earth becomes the less important part of the landscape because you find yourself constantly raising your eyes to look at the sky. In the arid landscape the sky is the final arbiter. When you have understood that, not intellectually but emotionally, you have also understood why it is that the great trinity of monotheistic religions, Judaism, Christianity and Islam, which removed the source of power from the earth itself to the spaces outside the earth, were evolved in desert regions. And of the three, Islam, perhaps because it is the most recently born, operates the most directly and with the greatest strength upon the daily actions of those who embrace it.

For a person born into a culture where religion has long ago become a thing quite separate from daily life, it is a startling experience to find himself suddenly in the midst of a culture where there is a minimum of discrepancy between dogma and natural behavior, and this is one of the great fascinations of being in North Africa. I am not speaking of Egypt, where the old harmony is gone, decayed from within. My own impressions of Egypt

Marrakesh—Berber tribesmen in regalia

before Nasser are those of a great panorama of sun-dried disintegration. In any case, she has had a different history from the rest of Mediterranean Africa, she is ethnically and linguistically distinct, and is more a part of the Levant than of the region we ordinarily mean when we speak of North Africa. But in Tunisia, Algeria and Morocco there are still people whose lives proceed according to the ancient pattern of concord between God and man, agreement between theory and practice, identity of word and flesh (or however one prefers to conceive and define that pristine state of existence we intuitively feel we once enjoyed and now have lost).

I don't claim that the Moslems of North Africa are a group of mystics, heedless of bodily comfort, interested only in the welfare of the spirit. If you have ever bought so much as an egg from one of them, you learned that they are quite able to fend for themselves when it comes to money matters. The spoiled strawberries are at the bottom of the basket, the pebbles inextricably mixed with the lentils and the water with the milk, the same as in many other parts of the world, with the difference that if you ask the price of an object in a rural market, they will reply, all in one breath: "Fifty, how much will you give?" I should say that in the realm of *béah o shri* (selling and buying; note that in their minds selling comes first), which is what they call business, they are surpassed only by the Hindus, who are less emotional about it and therefore more successful, and by the Chinese, acknowledged masters of the Oriental branch of the science of commerce.

In Morocco you go into a bazaar to buy a wallet, somehow find yourself being propelled toward the back room to look at antique brass and rugs, are presently seated with a glass of mint tea in your hand and a platter of pastries in your lap, while smiling gentlemen modeling ancient caftans and marriage robes parade in front of you, the salesman who greeted you at the door having completely vanished. Later on you may once again ask timidly to see the wallets, which you noticed on display near the entrance. Likely as not, you will be told that the man in charge of wallets is at the moment saying his prayers, but that he will soon be back, and in the meantime would you not be pleased to see some magnificent jewelry from the court of Moulay Ismail? Business is business and prayers are prayers, and both are a part of the day's work.

When I meet fellow Americans traveling about here in North Africa, I ask them: "What did you expect to find here?" Almost without exception, regardless of the way they express it, the answer, reduced to its simplest terms, is a sense of mystery. They expect mystery, and they find it, since fortunately it is a quality difficult to extinguish all in a moment. They find it in the patterns of sunlight filtering through the latticework that covers the *souks,* in the unexpected turnings and tunnels of the narrow streets, in the women whose features still go hidden beneath the *litham,* in the secretiveness of the architecture, which is such that even if the front door of a house is open, it is impossible to see inside. If they listen as well as look, they find it too in the song the lone camel driver sings by his fire before dawn, in the calling of the muezzins at night, when their voices are like bright beams of sound piercing the silence, and, most often, in the dry beat of the darabukka, the hand drum played by the women everywhere, in the great city houses and in the remotest tents of the wilderness.

It is a strange sensation, when you are walking alone in a still, dark street late at night, to come upon a pile of cardboard boxes soaked with rain, and, as you pass by it, to find yourself staring into the eyes of a man sitting upright behind it. A thief? A beggar? The night watchman of the quarter? A spy for the Secret Police?

You just keep walking, looking at the ground, hearing your footsteps echo between the walls of the deserted street. Into your head comes the idea that you may suddenly hear the sound of a conspiratorial whistle, and that something unpleasant may be about to happen. A little farther along you see,

Chez Ali—a nighttime display of Berber horsemanship and traditional feast

deep in the recess of an arcade of shops, another man reclining in a deck chair, asleep. Then you realize that all along the street there are men both sleeping and sitting quietly awake, and that even in the hours of its most intense silence the place is never empty of people.

It is only three years since the establishment of independence in Morocco, but already in each city there is a nucleus of younger Moslems who fraternize freely with the writers and painters (most of whom are American girls and boys) who have wandered into this part of the world and found it to their liking. Together they give very staid, quiet parties which show a curious blend of Eastern and Western etiquette. Usually no Moslem girls are present. Everyone will be stretched out on mattresses, and kif and hashish will be on hand, but half the foreigners will be sticking to their highballs. A good many paintings are looked at, and there is a lot of uninformed conversation about art and expression and religion. When food is passed around, the Moslems, for all their passionate devotion to European manners, not only adhere to their own custom of using chunks of bread to sop up the oily *mruq* at the bottom of their plates, but manage to impose it on the others as well, so that everybody is busy rubbing pieces of bread over his plate. Why not? The food is cooked to be eaten in that fashion, and is less tasty if eaten any other way.

Many of the Moslems paint too; after so many centuries of religious taboo with regard to the making of representational images, abstraction is their natural mode of expression. You can see in their canvases the elaboration of design worked out by the Berbers in their crafts: patterns that show constant avoidance of representation but manage all the same to suggest recognizable things. Naturally, their paintings are a great success with the visiting artists, who carry their admiration to the point of imitation. The beat-generation North Africans are music-mad, but they get their music via radio and phonograph. They are enthusiastic about the music of their own country, but unlike their fathers, they don't sing or play it. They are also fond of such exotic items as Congo drumming, the music of India, and particularly the more recent American jazz (Art Blakey, Chico Hamilton, Horace Silver).

At the moment, writing about any part of Africa is a little like trying to draw a picture of a roller coaster in motion. You can say: It *was* thus and so, or, it is *becoming* this or that, but you risk making a misstatement if you say categorically that anything *is*, because likely as not you will open tomorrow's newspaper to discover that it has changed. On the whole the new governments of Tunisia and Morocco are desirous of furthering tourism in their respective countries; they are learning that the average tourist is more interested in native dancing than in the new bus terminal; that he is more willing to spend money in the Casbah than to inspect new housing projects. For a while, after the demise of the violently unpopular Pasha of Marrakesh, Thami el Glaoui (one of whose sources of income was a percentage of the earnings of the twelve thousand prostitutes of his city), the great public square of Marrakesh, the Djemâa el-Fna, was used solely as a parking lot. Now, anyone who has visited the region will tell you that the biggest single attraction for tourists in all North Africa was the Djemâa el-Fna in Marrakesh. It was hard to find a moment of the day or night when tourists could not be found prowling around among its acrobats, singers, storytellers, snake charmers, dancers and medicine men. Without it Marrakesh became just another Moroccan city. And so the Djemâa el-Fna was reinstated, and now goes on more or less as before.

Both Tunisia's Bourghiba and Morocco's King Mohammed V are interested in retaining close ties with the West, but in order to ingratiate themselves with their constituents they find themselves obliged to make increasing numbers of concessions to its enemies within their own governments. The fate of both countries hangs upon the outcome of the war in Algeria. The longer France continues hostilities, the less likelihood there will be that any part of North Africa can remain within the orbit of the Western world. And doubtless France will continue to insist upon her "rights" in Algeria as long as we support her side in the struggle.

The political prospect for Barbary does not look bright—except to those who would like to see the neutralist bloc extended to the Atlantic coast. These latter people are likely to present the argument that such a development would be a natural one since the countries are Moslem and adhere to the Arab League. The point is that North Africa is inhabited, like Malaya and Pakistan, by Moslems who are not Arabs. *Encyclopaedia Britannica's*

estimate of the percentage of Arab stock in the population of Morocco dates from two decades ago, but there has been no influx of Arabs since. It gives 10 per cent as an approximate figure. The remaining 90 per cent of the people are Berbers, who anthropologically have nothing to do with the Arabs. They are not of Semitic origin, and have been living where they are since long before the Arab conquerors came.

Even after thirteen hundred years, the Berbers' conception of how to observe the Moslem religion is by no means identical with that of the descendants of the men who brought it to them. And, the city Moslems complain, they do not observe the fast of Ramadan properly; they neither veil nor segregate their women and, most objectionable of all, they have a passion for forming cults dedicated to the worship of local saints. In this their religious practices show a serious deviation from orthodoxy, inasmuch as during the *moussems*, those gigantic pilgrimages which are held periodically under the auspices of each particular brotherhood, men and women *together* dance themselves into a prolonged frenzy which can last for thirty-six hours at a stretch. Self-torture, the inducing of trances, ordeal by fire and the sword, and the eating of such delicacies as broken glass and scorpions are also usual on these occasions.

El Jadidah—washday

The traveler who has been present at one of these indescribable gatherings will never forget it, although if he dislikes the sight of blood and suffering, he will probably try hard to put it out of his mind. To me these spectacles are filled with great beauty, because their obvious purpose is to prove the superiority of the spirit over the flesh. The sight of ten or twenty thousand people actively declaring their faith, demonstrating en masse the power of that faith, can scarcely be anything but inspiring. You lie in the fire, I gash my legs and arms with a knife, he pounds a sharpened bone into his thigh with a rock—then, together, covered with ashes and blood, we sing and dance in joyous praise of the saint and the god who make it possible for us to triumph over pain and, by extension, over death itself. For the participants, of course, exhaustion and ecstasy are inseparable.

Moulay Idris—a street scene

This cult-worship, based on vestiges of an earlier religion, has long been frowned upon by the devout urban Moslems of North Africa, and as early as the mid-thirties various restrictions were placed on its practice. Now at last, all public manifestations of it have been effectively suppressed. There were several reasons why the educated Moslems objected to the brotherhoods. During the periods of the protectorates in Tunisia and Morocco, the colonial administrations did not hesitate to use them for their own political ends, to ensure more complete domination. Also, it has always been felt that visitors who happened to witness the members of a cult in action were given an unfortunate impression of cultural backwardness. Most important was the fact that the rituals were unorthodox and thus unacceptable to true Moslems. If you mentioned such cults as the Hamatcha, the Derqaoua, the Aissaoua, the Haddaoua, the Jilala or the Gnaoua to a city man, he invariably cried: "They're all criminals! They should be put in jail!" without stopping to reflect that it would be difficult to incarcerate more than half the population of any country. I think one reason why the city folk are so violent about the cults is that most of them are only one generation removed from connection with them themselves and, knowing the official attitude toward them, feel a certain guilt at being even that much involved with them. Having been born into a family of adepts is not a thing anyone can quickly forget. Each brotherhood has its own songs and drum rhythms, immediately recognizable as such by persons both within and outside the group. In early childhood rhythmical patterns and sequences of tones become a part of an adept's subconscious, and in later life it is not difficult to attain the trance state when one hears them again.

One of my acquaintances, who has always been vociferous in his denunciation of the brotherhoods, eventually admitted to me that all the older members of his family were adherents to the Jilala cult, citing immediately afterward as an example of their perniciousness an experience of his grandmother some three years before. Like the rest of the family, she was brought up as a Jilalía, but was too old to take part in the observances, which nowadays are held secretly. One evening she was alone in the house, her children and grandchildren having all gone to the movies, and since she had nothing else to do, she went to bed. Somewhere nearby, there was a meeting of Jilala; the drums penetrated her dreams, and in her sleep she rose and, in her night clothing, made her way toward the sounds. She was found next morning unconscious in a vegetable garden near the house where the meeting had taken place, having been badly bitten by ants. The reason she fell, the family assured me, was that at a certain moment the drumming had stopped; if it had gone on, she would have arrived. The drummers always continue until everyone has been brought out of his trance.

"But they did not know she was coming," they said, "and so the next morning, after we had carried her home we had to send for the drummers to bring her to her senses."

This is the sort of story that infuriates the younger generation of French-educated Moslems if they hear it being told to foreigners. And for the latter to be interested in such things upsets them even more. "Are all the people in your country Holy Rollers?" they demand. "Why don't you write about the civilized people here, instead of the most backward?"

I understand them. They would like to see themselves presented to the outside world in the most "advanced" light possible. They find it perverse of a Westerner to be interested only in the dissimilarities between their culture and his. However, that's the way some of us Westerners are.

Not long ago I wrote on the character of the North Africa Moslem. An illiterate Moroccan friend wanted to know what was in it, and so, in a running translation into Moghrebi, I read him certain passages. His comment was terse: "That's shameful."

"Why?" I demanded.

"Because you've written about people just as they are."

"For us that's not shameful."

"For us it is. You've made us like animals. You've said that few of us can read and write."

"Isn't that true?"

"Of course not! We can all read and write, just like you. And we would—if only we'd had lessons."

I thought this interesting and told it to a Moslem lawyer, assuming it would amuse him. It didn't. "He's quite right," he announced. "Truth is not what you perceive with your senses, but what you feel in your heart."

"But there is such a thing as objective truth!" I cried. "Or don't you attach importance to that?"

He smiled tolerantly. "Not in the way you do, for its own sake. That is statistical truth. We are interested in that, yes, but only as a means of getting to the real truth underneath. For us there is very little visible truth in the world these days." However specious this kind of talk may seem, it is still clear to me that the lawyer was voicing a feeling common to the great mass of city dwellers here, educated or not.

With an estimated adult illiteracy rate of 80 to 90 per cent, perhaps the greatest need for all of North Africa is universal education. So far there has been a very small amount, and as we ourselves say, a little learning is a dangerous thing. The Europeans always have been guilty of massive neglect with regard to schools for the Moslems in their North African possessions. In time, their shortsighted policy is likely to prove the heaviest handicap of all in the desperate attempt of the present rulers to keep the region within the Western sphere of influence. The task of educating these people is not made easier by the fact that Moghrebi, the language of the majority, is purely a spoken tongue, and that for reading and writing they must resort to Standard Arabic, which is as far from their idiom as Latin is from Italian. But slowly the transition is taking place. If you sit in a Moroccan café at the hour of a news broadcast, the boy fanning the fire will pause with the bellows in his hand, the card players lay down their cards, the talkers cease to argue as the announcer begins to speak, and an expression of ferocious intensity appears on every countenance. Certainly they are vitally interested in what is being said, for they are aware of their own increasing importance in the world pattern, but the almost painful expressions are due to each man's effort to understand the words of Standard Arabic as they come over the air. Afterward, there is often an argument as to exactly what was said.

"The British are at war with Yemen for being friendly to Gamal Abdel Nasser."

"You're crazy. He said Gamal Abdel Nasser is making war against Yemen because the British are there."

"No. He said Gamal Abdel Nasser *will* make war against Yemen if they let the British in."

"No, no! Against the *British* if they send guns to Yemen."

This state of affairs, if it does not keep all members of the populace accurately informed, at least has the advantage of increasing their familiarity with the language their children are learning in school.

There is a word which non-Moslems invariably use to describe Moslems in general: fanatical. As though the word could not be applied equally well to any group of people who care deeply about anything! Just now, the North African Moslems are passionately involved in proving to themselves that they are of the same stature as Europeans. The attainment of political independence is only one facet of their problem. The North African knows that, when it comes to appreciating his culture, the average tourist cannot go much farther toward understanding it than a certain condescending curiosity. He realizes that, at best, to the European he is merely picturesque. Therefore, he reasons, to be taken seriously he must cease being picturesque. Traditional customs, clothing and behavior must be replaced by something unequivocally European. In this he is fanatical. It does not occur to him that what he is rejecting is authentic and valid, and that what he is taking on is meaningless imitation. And if it did occur to him, it wouldn't matter in the least. This total indifference to the cultural heritage everywhere appears to be a necessary adjunct to the early stages of nationalism.

Hospitality in North Africa knows no limits. You are taken in and treated as a member of the family. If you don't enjoy yourself, it is not your host's fault, but rather the result of your own inadaptability, for every attempt is made to see that you are happy and comfortable. Some time ago I was

the guest of two brothers who had an enormous house in the medina of Fez. So that I should feel truly at home, I was given an entire wing of the establishment, a tiled patio with a room on either side and a fountain in the center. There were great numbers of servants to bring me food and drink, and also to inquire, before my hosts came to call, whether I was disposed to receive them. When they came they often brought singers and musicians to entertain me. The only hitch was that they went to such lengths to treat me as one of them that they also assumed I was not interested in going out into the city. During the entire fortnight I spent with them I never once found my way out of the house, or even out of my own section of it, since all doors were kept locked and bolted, and only the guard, an old Senegalese slave, had the keys. For long hours I sat in the patio listening to the sounds of the city outside, sometimes hearing faint strains of music that I would have given anything really to hear, watching the square of deep-blue sky above my head slowly become a softer and lighter blue as twilight approached, waiting for the swallows that wheeled above the patio when the day was finally over and the muezzins began their calls to evening prayer, and merely existing in the hope that someone would come, something would happen before too many more hours had gone past. But as I say, if I was bored, that was my own fault and not theirs. They were doing everything that they could to please me.

Just as in that twelfth-century fortress in Fez I had been provided with a small hand-wound phonograph and one record (Josephine Baker singing *J'ai Deux Amours*, a song hit of that year), so all over North Africa you are confronted with a mélange of the very old and the most recent, with no hint of anything left over from the intervening centuries. It is one of the great charms of the place, the fact that your today carries with it no memories of yesterday or the day before; everything that is not medieval is completely new. The younger generation of French and Jews, born and raised in the cities of North Africa, for the most part have no contact at all with that which is ancient in their countries. A Moroccan girl whose family moved from Rabat to New York, upon being asked what she thought of her new home, replied: "Well, of course, coming from a new country as I do, it's very hard to get used to all these old houses here in New York. I had no idea New York was so *old.*" It is hard to remember that the French began to settle in Morocco only at the time of World War I, and that the mushroom cities of Casablanca, Agadir and Tangier grew up in the thirties. Xauen, whose mountains are visible from the terrace of my apartment in Tangier, was entered by European troops in 1920. Even in southern Algeria, where one is inclined to think of the French as having been stationed for a much longer time, there are war monuments bearing battle dates as recent as 1912. Throughout the whole first quarter of the century the North African frontier was continuously being pushed southward by means of warfare, and south of the Grand Atlas it was 1936 before "pacification" came to an end and European civilians were allowed, albeit on the strict terms laid down by the military, to look for the first time into the magic valleys of the Drân, the Dadès and the Todra.

Appearing unexpectedly in out-of-the-way regions of North Africa has never been without its difficulties. I remember making an impossible journey before the last war in a produce truck over the Grand Atlas to Ouarzazat, full of excitement at the prospect of seeing the Casbah with its strange painted towers, only to be forced to remain three days inside the shack that passed for a hotel, and then sent on another truck straight back to Marrakesh, having seen nothing but Foreign Legionnaires, and having heard no music other than the bugle calls that issued every so often from the nearby camp. Another time I entered Tunisia on camel back from across the Great Eastern Erg. I had two camels and one hard-working camel driver, whose job it was to run all day long from one beast to the other and try, by whacking their hind legs, to keep them walking in something resembling a straight line. This was a much more difficult task than it sounds; although our course was generally due east, one of the animals had an inexplicable desire to walk southward, while the other was possessed by an equally mysterious urge to go north. The poor man passed his time screaming: "*Hut! Aïda!*" and trying to run both ways at once. His turban was continually coming unwound, and he had no time to attend to the scarf he was knitting, in spite of the fact that he kept the yarn and needles dangling around his neck, ready to work on at any moment.

We did finally cross the border and amble into Tunisia, where we were immediately apprehended by the police. The camel driver was sent back to Algeria where he belonged, and I started on my painful way up through Tunisia, where the French authorities evidently had decided to make my stay in the country as wretched as possible. In the oasis at Nefta, in the hotel at Tozeur, even in the Mosque of Sidi Oqba at Kairouan, I was arrested and lugged off to the commissariat, carefully questioned, and told that I need not imagine I could make a move of which they would not be fully aware.

The explanation was that in spite of my American passport they were convinced I was a German; in those days anybody wandering around North Africa who was not an obvious tourist was suspect. Even the Moslems looked at me closely and said: "*Toi pas Français. Toi Allemand,*" to which I never replied, for fear of having to pay the price that would have been demanded if my true status had been revealed to them.

Algeria is a country where it is better to keep moving around than to stay long in one place. Its towns are not very interesting, but its landscapes are impressive. In the winter, traveling by train across the western steppes, you can go all day and see nothing but flat stretches of snow on all sides, unrelieved by trees in the foreground or by mountains in the distance. In the summer these same desolate lands are cruelly hot, and the wind swirls the dust into tall yellow pillars that move deliberately from one side of the empty horizon to the other. When you come upon a town in such regions, lying like the remains of a picnic lunch in the middle of an endless parking lot, you know it was the French who put it there. The Algerians prefer to live along the wild and beautiful seacoast, in the palm gardens of the south, atop the cliffs bordering the dry rivers, or on the crests of the high mountains in the center of the country. Up there above the slopes dotted with almond trees, the Berber villages sit astride the long spines of the lesser ranges. The men and women file down the zigzagging paths to cultivate the rich valleys below, here and there in full view of the snowfields where the French have built their skiing resorts. Far to the south lie the parallel chains of red sawtooth mountains which run northeast to southwest across the entire country and divide the plains from the desert. It is at this natural frontier that Algeria proper ends. For administrative reasons the French originally decided that Algeria was to include the desert itself, straight down to French West Africa, but recently a border was created and a new political entity called simply "*Le Sahara,*" came into being. Here, sheltered from Algerian guerrilla bands, the French hope to conduct their own nuclear tests.

From the point of view of the onlookers here, the crucial Algerian struggle is to the 'fifties rather what the Spanish Civil War was to the 'thirties. Friendships break up as a result of bitter arguments, and the same old epithets of "Fascist" and "Communist" are tossed back and forth. But regardless of how the tragic episode terminates, no part of North Africa will again be the same sort of paradise for Europeans that it was during the past fifty years. The place has been thrown open to the twentieth century. With Europeanization and nationalism have come a consciousness of identity and the awareness of that identity's commercial possibilities. From now on the North Africans, like the Mexicans, will control and exploit their own charms, rather than being placed on exhibit for us by their managers, and the result will be a very different thing. Tourist land it is still, and doubtless will continue to be for a while, and it is on that basis only that we as residents or intending visitors are now obliged to consider it. We now come here as paying guests of the inhabitants themselves rather than of their exploiters. Travel here is certain not to be so easy or so comfortable as before, and prices are ten times higher than they were, but at least we meet the people on terms of equality, which, we must admit, is a healthier situation.

If you live long enough in a place where the question of colonialism versus self-government is constantly being discussed, you are bound to find yourself having a very definite opinion on the subject. The difficulty is that some of your coresidents feel one way and some the other, but all feel

strongly. Those in favor of colonialism argue that you can't "give" (quotes mine) an almost totally illiterate people political power and expect them to create a democracy, and that is doubtless true; but the point is that since they are inevitably going to take the power sooner or later, it is only reasonable to help them take it while they still have at least some measure of good will toward their erstwhile masters. The die-hard French attitude is summed up in a remark made to me by a friendly immigration officer at the Algiers airport. "Our great mistake," he said sadly, "was ever to allow these savages to learn to read and write." I said I supposed that was logical, if one expected to rule forever, which I knew, given the intelligence of the French, they did not intend to do, since it was impossible. The official ceased looking sad and became much less friendly.

At a dinner in Marrakesh during the French occupation, the Frenchman sitting beside me became engaged in an amicable discussion with a Moroccan across the table. "But look at the facts, *mon cher ami.* Before our arrival there was constant warfare between the tribes. Since we came the population of Morocco has doubled. Is that true or not?"

The Moroccan leaned forward. "We can take care of our own births and deaths," he said, smiling. "If we must be killed, just let other Moroccans attend to it. We really prefer that."

Right: Marrakesh—a woman's hand decorated with henna

WHAT'S SO DIFFERENT ABOUT MARRAKESH

Marrakesh, with its encircling oasis, was the idea of Yusuf ibn Tashfin, a Saharan chieftain of the eleventh century. The site was a treeless plain, flat as a table, some 35 miles from the northern flanks of the High Atlas. It was natural that he should have imported the date palm, which any Saharan considers the only true tree, and used it to transform the empty wasteland into a vast palm grove. The miles of enclosing ramparts were built, the mosques and markets established, and Yussuf ibn Tashfin went on to glorify the name of Allah in Spain. He had left behind a work of art—a city of noble proportions and spectacular beauty.

What is astonishing is the fact that after 900 hard years (for life in Morocco has seldom proceeded smoothly) the beauty should still be so evident and so dazzling. Part of the reason is that, as they worked, the builders of the city saw each garden, terrace and pool in relation to the long chain of snowy peaks behind it.

In Marrakesh more than in other cities, the eye is continually being encouraged to contemplate that which is far away. Automatically it follows the line of the ramparts to the empty plain, coming to rest on the most distant vista. The mountains are so much a part of the scene that on the days when they are invisible the city seems incomplete. Contemporary Moroccans feel much the same about the peaks of the Atlas as their forebears. In my drives around the city, each time my chauffeur looks up and sees them shining and white against the sky, he sighs and says, "Look at the works of God!"

When I first came here, camels ambled through the back alleys of the medina, and 12,000 girls lived inside the walls of the Quartier Réservé, ready to provide amusement for their prospective clients. The camels are restricted to the country now, and the Quartier has long since been razed. Otherwise the character of Marrakesh is little changed.

What is different is the tempo of life. The era of the automobile has finally arrived, and the aim of every Marrakchi is to own one. Thousands already do; the rest use motorcycles and bicycles and live in hope. Bicycle riders are in the great majority. They are the natural enemy of the pedestrian. He who dares walk finds that there is no safe place for him; in the narrowest alley he can suddenly be run down by someone coming along silently from behind. Since it is impossible to see the medina save on foot, visitors find themselves obliged to be constantly on the lookout.

Being in Marrakesh in winter, if there is sun, is a little like standing in front of a fireplace: You are hot on one side and cold on the other. If there is no sun, you are cold on both sides. The changes in temperature between day and night are impressive.

Right: Marrakesh—a street in the wool dyers' market   *Following page: Marrakesh—in the stall of a copper and brass merchant*

Winter is the high season, but spring and autumn are far more pleasant. As for the summer, it is the favorite season of many foreign residents, in spite of the temperature, which goes above 120 degrees in the shade during an east wind. But to be comfortable under such conditions one must be living at home, not in hotels. Not having a house in Marrakesh, I generally stay away from it between June and September.

Surprisingly, when the French arrived in 1912 their take-over did not cause any great changes in the aspect of the medina. Following the pattern established by Marshal Lyautey, they left it intact and built their own town, El Gueliz, two miles away to the west. Now that the two nuclei have more or less grown together—without, however, confusing their respective identities—it is clear that here is by far the most successful example of French city-planning in Morocco. The landscape gardening throughout the city is superb, and while one may have reservations about the extensive use of floodlighting, there is no denying that the ramparts are dramatic when bathed in their gold light.

One of the great touristic pleasures of Marrakesh is to take a horse-drawn carriage at sunset and drive the seven and a half miles around the periphery of the medina, following the line of the ramparts and watching the bisque-pink walls and bastions as their color is modified by the changing light.

The Djemâa el-Fna is probably the most fascinating open square in the world. Every afternoon all Marrakesh comes here as to a fair. On a sample afternoon one can watch some expert Sudanese dancing by a troupe of Gnaoua, a troupe of acrobats, Jilala drinking boiling water, Aissaoua charming cobras and vipers, trained monkeys, and a Surrealist act by two Haddaoua seated on carpets surrounded by plastic flowers and live pigeons.

At a certain point in the Haddaoua's routine one of the men beckons to a pigeon, which comes to him and perches on his shoulder. Then he orders the bird to go across the square to the Banque du Maroc and steal some banknotes. The pigeon flies over to the bank and alights above the entrance door, looking warily down at the armed guards standing there. Soon it returns to the man's shoulder, where it appears to be whispering into his ear. "What? No money?" cries the man. "How are we going to eat?" Meanwhile his partner has been intoning pious phrases, preparatory to going around the circle of watchers and taking up a collection.

During recent decades, as the population has grown and property values have increased, the Djemâa el-Fna has constantly been reduced in size.

A police station has been built, space has been allotted for carriage and taxi stands, and long rows of stalls have been set up on two sides of the square. This year a sizable section of the east end has been cut off, to be used as a parking space for several thousand bicycles, and still another row of stalls constructed. Were it not for the fact that the Djemâa el-Fna is the number one tourist attraction of Morocco, the authorities undoubtedly would have done away with it.

In the late fifties, Eleanor Roosevelt was in Marrakesh as the guest of His Majesty Mohammed V. At dinner the first night, Mrs. Roosevelt confided to her host that the one place she always visited when she came to Marrakesh was the Djemâa el-Fna; she could hardly wait to see it again, she added. Regretfully the king told her that the square had been converted into a parking lot. When she heard this, her disappointment was so intense that the king promised to reinstate the institution at the earliest opportunity. He did so, and it has functioned in its traditional fashion ever since.

Behind the Djemâa el-Fna is a quarter generally referred to as "the bazaars." Until 1961 the streets here were covered with cane lattice work, an attractive architectural formula, but one which caused the destruction of the entire section. About 500 shops were gutted that summer by a fire which started in a chickpea-roasting stall. Rebuilding has been done in metal—less picturesque but more likely to preserve the few valuable objects that survived the holocaust. Beyond the bazaars are the *souks*. Each *souk* consists of many stalls selling the same kind of merchandise, which is often being made on the premises in full view of the buyer. Here prices are lower and there is more variety to choose from, but purchasing takes correspondingly longer.

There is generally considered to be only one *hôtel de grand luxe* in Morocco, and that is the Mamounia of Marrakesh. I think of luxury in terms of comfort, service and privacy, while those who run today's hotels would appear to conceive it in terms of swimming pools, saunas and air-conditioning units. Perhaps that is why the Mamounia's luxury now seems largely vestigial, a nostalgic reminder of the era not too long ago when Winston Churchill came each winter to sit painting in the garden.

The Mamounia is still the biggest and best—there is no doubt of that—and if you are fortunate enough to get a room with a southern exposure you have an unparalleled view of the famous olive grove and the Atlas. Among the more recently built hotels are the Es Saadi, by the Casino, the Almoravides, just inside Bab Doukkala, and the Menara, about halfway between the medina and the modern quarter of El Gueliz. These are all first-class establishments. There are also two new American-style motels, both on the Avenue de la Menara, outside the city. Several more hotels are under construction at the moment, including an enormous Club Méditerranée directly on the Djemâa el-Fna. However, the more room they make for visitors, the more visitors there are. Residents speak glumly of a saturation point, but so far there is no sign of such a thing.

Night life as we conceive it is not a part of the mores of the land; what little is provided has been arranged specifically for tourists, and is therefore not of much interest. Entertainment with dinner, however, is another matter. Often one can find some of the best Moroccan musicians and dancers at the large tourist restaurants of the medina that specialize in local dishes. The Gharnatta, the Ksar-el-Hamra, and the Dar-es-Salaam are spacious, elaborate establishments where the accent is on atmosphere and entertainment rather than food.

Moroccan cooking is at last beginning to be known and appreciated by Americans. Every gastronome who comes to Morocco should learn during his stay how to make at least one Moroccan dish. In any case he will want the experience of tasting the most delectable samples of *cuisine marocaine* to be had anywhere, and he will find them at La Maison Arabe just inside the huge arched gate of Bab Doukkala. He must remember to make his reservation at least a day in advance, and he must be so devoted to the art of eating that he is not disturbed by the severity of the *patronne* and the almost monastic atmosphere.

The resident expatriate colony is smaller than reports might lead one to believe. The Comtesse de Breteuil lives in the famous Villa Taylor which housed Roosevelt and Churchill during World War II; this is the hub of what social life exists in Marrakesh. The Getty house is a brilliant example of the glamour that can be created by stringing together a number of old houses. Arndt von Bohlen (heir to the Krupp empire) has a large estate just to the west of El Gueliz, outside the city. Yves Saint Laurent a few years ago bought a beautiful little house which he uses strictly as a retreat from the rigors of life in Paris. The house was designed by its original owner, whose brother Prince Doan Vihn na Champaçak recently gave up his quiet life as a painter here in Marrakesh to marry Barbara Hutton. Ira Belline, costume designer for Diaghileff and Jouvet, the niece of Igor Stravinsky, has lived for a good many years in the oasis, several miles out of town. The American writer John Hopkins has an adobe house among the palm trees on this property.

The most recent addition to the colony of homeowners is Pierre Balmain. There are American and European residents in hidden corners throughout the medina, living quietly in their rebuilt Moroccan houses. The architectural transformations seldom affect the outer wall of a house, so that it is impossible to tell from the street whether Moroccans or foreigners live there.

The only Americans visible to the naked eye are the temporary visitors, who can be subdivided into tourists and those whom the Moroccans call the *hippiyine*, (feminine singular *hippiya*, with the accent on the second syllable). As might be expected, the natives here find the hippie phenomenon very difficult to understand. Their reactions, which initially were favorable, have been modified by several years of contact with members of the movement and are now at best ambivalent, and often frankly fearful. The authorities are worried that the attitude of disrespect for the law shown by some hippies may infect young Moroccans who fraternize with them. A good number of local youths now carefully cultivate the hippie look. There have been public campaigns against long hair and eccentric clothing with mobile guards roaming the cities, but these tactics have not had an appreciable effect.

Last year the large Café du Glacier on the Djemâa el-Fna teemed with young travelers wearing beards, chains, parkas, tchamiras, djellabas, R' Guibat rezzas, and a whole assortment of African accouterments. This year it is frequented only by Moroccans and stray tourists. The Friends of the

Right: Marrakesh—the courtyard of the Medersa Ben Youssef

World have opted for secrecy and have abandoned the big public places in favor of tiny, hidden stalls in the back alleys where the tourists are unable to find them. For, in the past years, the hippies have become a principal tourist attraction of Marrakesh.

At the age of 20, I was here in Marrakesh, without drugs and fancy dress, it is true, but living in very much the same fashion as the hippies live here today, showing scorn for that which was familiar and boundless enthusiasm for everything Moroccan. The principal difference between us is that they, traveling in numbers and having no self-consciousness, are not satisfied with being spectators; they want to participate. It is as if they thought that if they try hard and long enough, they will become Moroccans themselves.

Sometimes at night as you walk through the Djemâa el-Fna you come upon a circle of seated, burnoose-clad figures. In the center there will be two or three Moroccans playing on drums. Upon examination one circle turns out to be composed of Americans, sitting in religious silence while their heads respond in spastic movements to the rhythm of the drums. Participation at such a basic level, while not likely to lead to further understanding between the two cultures, is a harmless enough activity, and certainly a more meaningful one than the tourist custom of sitting in a nightclub whose every detail has been planned in anticipation of Western tastes. Now Moroccan girls are being trained to become belly dancers—a hitherto unheard-of thing in Morocco. But since that is what tourists are said to want, that is what they get.

Inaccurate information is responsible for the disappointments of most travelers. I have known people to return from their first visit to Marrakesh and express surprise, if not chagrin, at finding the city so open and accessible. It had no mystery. But no one ever claimed that Marrakesh was mysterious, I tell them. During the time of the Protectorate, in their touristic propaganda the French were quite explicit about it. Assuming that "mystery" was furnished by such conventional items as winding tunnels, narrow alleys and eyes peering from behind latticed peepholes, they reserved the word for descriptions of Fez. It was *"Fès la mystérieuse"*; Marrakesh was strictly *"la Rouge."*

If one stays in a city for any length of time, one discovers that its general atmosphere depends largely upon the attitude of its inhabitants. The Marrakchis themselves can be quite as baffling to the visitor as any succession of tunnels and alleys. They love to engage in strange little games with foreigners—games in which often they have nothing whatever to gain, unless it be the expressions of bewilderment and frustration they can call forth on the foreigners' faces. For the visitor, Marrakesh is a constant confrontation with the unlikely, outlandish and absurd.

For example, I enter a restaurant not far from the Djemâa el-Fna, sit down and ask for the *carte* and the *menu*. There are no prices mentioned on either. I call the attention of the waiter to the oversight. He says airily: "You order what you like and I'll charge what I like."

I am sitting in a café in Gueliz. A taxi drives up, and a little man gets out. He is about three feet high, with a huge head and practically no legs. He pays the driver and comes tottering directly to the *terrasse* of the café, where he begins to go from table to table asking for alms. I am wondering why he took no pains to hide his mode of arrival, and I ask him about it. "I always take taxis," he says proudly. "I have plenty of money." Perhaps he sees incredulity in my face, for he goes on. "I have three houses and a store in the medina." It takes me a moment to digest this information. "But then," I begin hesitantly, "why don't you just sit at a table like everyone else?" His hand is still out. "That's no good," he says. "I want to know what's going on. I go to *all* the cafés." I give him the coin I have been holding in my hand, and he waddles on.

For those spending the season in Marrakesh, the two most popular places to visit nearby are Essaouira and Oukaimeden, where the activities are respectively sea-bathing and skiing. Essaouira, 125 miles due west of Marrakesh, is on a spit of land jutting out into the Atlantic. It is one of the most attractive small towns in all North Africa, as yet unspoiled, with a wide sandy beach that stretches south as far as the eye can see.

Oukaimeden, at an altitude of 8,399 feet, nestles below the peak of Djebel Toubkal (13,665 feet) and advertises the highest ski lift in Africa. (I am curious to see the list of African ski lifts.) The drive through the valleys and gorges is beautiful, and the food is excellent. Skiers often stay on until April.

Marrakesh—a waterseller in the Djemâa el-Fna

Marrakesh—courtyard of the Saadian tombs

Marrakesh—tombs of the Saadian kings, built by Ahmed Edh Dahabi in the sixteenth century

THE SECRET SAHARA

Immediately when you arrive in the Sahara, for the first or the tenth time, you notice the stillness. An incredible, absolute silence prevails outside the towns, and within, even in busy places like the markets, there is a hushed quality in the air, as if the quiet were a conscious force which, resenting the intrusion of sound, minimizes and disperses it straightway. Then there is the sky, compared to which all other skies seem fainthearted efforts. Solid and luminous, it is always the focal point of the landscape. At sunset, the precise, curved shadow of the earth rises into it swiftly from the horizon, cutting it into light section and dark section. When all daylight is gone, and the space is thick with stars, it is still of an intense and burning blue, darkest directly overhead and paling toward the earth, so that the night never grows really dark.

You leave the gate of the fort or the town behind, pass the camels lying outside, go up into the dunes, or out onto the hard, stony plain and stand a while, alone. Presently, you will either shiver and hurry back inside the walls, or you will go on standing there and let something very peculiar happen to you, something that everyone who lives there has undergone, and which the French call "the baptism of solitude." It is a unique sensation, and it has nothing to do with loneliness, for loneliness presupposes memory. Here, in this wholly mineral landscape lighted by stars like flares, even memory disappears; nothing is left but your own breathing and the sound of your heart beating. A strange, and by no means pleasant, process of reintegration begins inside you, and it remains to be seen whether you will fight against it, and insist on remaining the person you have always been, or whether you will let it take its course. For no one who has stayed in the Sahara for a while is quite the same as when he came. But it is an interesting commentary on both the desert and the French, who among European peoples principally inhabit it, that the net result of their mingling has generally been a distinct underlining of the human virtues.

There is a wonderful feeling of friendly sympathy in the Sahara; it is like a small unspoiled rural community where everyone respects the rights of everyone else. Each time you live there a while, and leave it, you are struck with the indifference and impersonality of the world outside. If, during your travels there, you forget something, you will find it later on your way back; the idea of stealing it will not have occurred to anyone. You can wander where you like, out in the wilderness or in the darkest alleys of the towns—no one will molest you.

As yet, no members of the indigent, wandering, unwanted proletariat from northern Algeria have come down here, because there is nothing to attract them. Almost everyone owns a parcel of land in an oasis and lives by working it. In the shade of the date palms wheat, barley and corn are grown, and these plants provide the staple items of diet. There are, usually, two or three Arab or Negro shopkeepers who sell things like sugar, tea, candles, matches, carbide for lighting, and cheap European cotton goods. In the larger towns there is sometimes a shop kept by a European, but the goods for sale are the same, because the customers are virtually all natives. Almost without exception, the only Europeans who live in the Sahara are the military and the ecclesiastic.

As a rule, the military and their aides are friendly men, agreeable to be with, interested in showing visitors everything worth seeing in their districts. This is fortunate, as the traveler is often completely at their mercy. He may have to depend on them for his food and lodging, for in the smaller places there are no hotels. He will probably have to depend on them for contact with the outside world, since anything he wants, like cigarettes or wine,

Eastern Sahara—desert sands at dawn

will have to be brought by truck from the military post, and his mail will have to be sent in care of the post. Also, it is up to the military to decide whether he shall have permission to move about freely in the region. The power to grant these privileges is vested in, let us say, one lonely lieutenant who lives two hundred miles from his nearest countryman, eats badly (anathema to any Frenchman) and wishes that neither camels, date palms, nor inquisitive foreigners had ever been created. Still, it is very rare to find an indifferent or unhelpful commandant. He is likely to invite you for drinks and dinner, show you the curiosities he has collected during his years in the *bled,* ask you to accompany him on his tours of inspection, or even to spend a fortnight with him and his *peloton* of several dozen native *meharistes* when they go out into the desert to make topographical surveys. Then you will be given your own camel—not an ambling pack camel that has to be driven with a stick by someone walking beside it, but a swift, trained animal that obeys the slightest tug of the reins.

But if the soldiers are agreeable, the priests, the Pères Blancs, are unforgettable. These White Fathers are exceptional men, intelligent and educated. There is no element of resignation in their eagerness to spend the remainder of their lives in distant outposts, dressed as Arabs, speaking Arabic, living in the rigorous, comfortless manner of the desert natives. They make no converts, and never expect to make any. "We are here only to show the Moslem that the Christian can be worthy of respect," they explain. The Arabic saying is that although the Christians are masters of the earth, the Moslems are the masters of Heaven; and for the military it is quite enough that the native recognize European supremacy on earth. Naturally, the White Fathers are not satisfied with that. They insist on proving to the inhabitants that the Christian can lead as exemplary a life as the most ardent follower of Mohammed. The austerity of the Fathers' mode of life inspires the native with true respect. And, as a result of the years spent in the desert among the natives, the Fathers have acquired a certain healthy and rather unorthodox fatalism, which is an excellent adjunct to their spiritual equipment, and a necessary one in dealing with the men among whom they have come to live.

In Adrar, I used to call on Père Geoffroy every afternoon. Sitting over glasses of mint tea, we would have long literary discussions. Down there, in the middle of the Sahara, he was as conversant with the latest books of Sartre and Camus as if he had been living in the shadow of Notre Dame de Paris. On my showing a reasonable astonishment, not only at that but at his willingness to read books of which he necessarily disapproved, he smiled and said, "One has to separate manner from matter, you know." And a visiting Father from El Goléa added, "We're the intellectuals of the desert, after all." Generous, tolerant and wise, they know the desert and its inhabitants as few travelers ever do.

With an area considerably larger than that of the United States, the Sahara is a continent within a continent, a skeleton, if you like, but still a separate entity from the rest of Africa which surrounds it. It has its own mountain ranges, rivers, lakes and forests, but they are largely vestigial. The mountain ranges have been reduced to gigantic bouldery bumps that rise above the neighboring countryside like the mountains on the moon. Some of the rivers appear as such for perhaps one day a year—others much less often. The lakes are of solid salt, and the forests have long since petrified. But the physical contours of the landscape vary as much as they do anywhere else. There are plains, hills, valleys, gorges, rolling lands, rocky peaks and volcanic craters—all without vegetation or even soil, properly speaking. Yet, probably the only parts that are monotonous to the eye are regions like the Tanezrouft, south of Reggan, a stretch of about five hundred miles of absolutely flat, gravel-strewn terrain, without the slightest sign of life, not the smallest undulation in the land, nothing to vary the implacable line of the horizon on all sides. After two days of this, the sight of even a rock in the distance awakens an emotion in the traveler; he feels like crying, "Land!"

Geographically speaking, most of Egypt is, of course, included in the Sahara, but the Nile has given her a history so utterly different from that of the rest of the desert that she cannot be considered culturally or economically a part of the Sahara. The civilization of Egypt has always been essentially

Above: Tiznit—entrance of the Grand Mosque

Following pages: Eastern Sahara—a Berber tribesman watering camels at the oasis of Merzouga

107

an urban one. When the rustic arrived at the city gates he hoped to be treated kindly. In the rest of the Sahara, it is quite the opposite. There it is the town-dweller who has always been the bumpkin, preyed upon by the nomad slicker. The rest of the Sahara, with the exception of the Fezzan (which was taken from Italy during World War II) and the relatively small Spanish colony of Rio de Oro on the Atlantic, is all under French command: Mauretania, the Hoggar, Tibesti, and the region of the dunes, which is roughly the farthest north.

As far into the past as our knowledge can reach, the Sahara has been inhabited by man. Most of the other animals, whose abode it formerly was, have become extinct there. If we believe the evidence of cave drawings, we can be sure that the giraffe, the hippopotamus and the rhinoceros were once dwellers of the region. The lion has disappeared in our own time, likewise the ostrich. Now and then, a crocodile is still discovered in some distant, hidden oasis pool, but the occurrence is so rare that when it happens it is a great event. The camel, of course, is not a native of Africa at all, but an importation from Asia, having arrived about the time of the end of the Roman Empire—about when the last elephants were killed off. Large numbers of the herds of wild elephants that roamed the northern reaches of the desert, in what is now Algeria, were captured and trained for use in the Carthaginian army, but it was the Romans who finally annihilated the species to supply ivory for the European market.

Fortunately for man, who seems to insist on continuing to live in surroundings which become increasingly inhospitable to him, gazelles are still plentiful, and there are, paradoxically enough, various kinds of edible fish in the water holes—often more than a hundred feet deep—throughout the Sahara. Certain species which abound in artesian wells are blind, having always lived deep in the subterranean lakes.

And so, the elephants and the Romans disappear, and the camels and the Arabs enter upon the scene. But, in between, a strange phenomenon occurs: a tribe of partially Judaized nomadic Berbers—the Zenata—spreads west and south from Eastern Algeria in a concerted effort that is unique in Berber history, and conquers the greater part of North Africa. When, later, the Arabs arrive with their new faith, the Zenata mostly fall back into the customary role of the conquered, assimilated Berbers, and adopt Islam as their own. In the cities, they go further and pretend to identify themselves racially with the conquerors from the East, so as to free themselves from the social stigma of being "natives." But to this day, there are living reminders of the time when the Zenata ruled the land; there are whole regions whose villages are inhabited principally by Berbers who still cling to the Jewish faith and costume. And, deep in the Sahara, near Adrar, is Tamentit, which was the center of a Jewish kingdom that, the year Columbus discovered America, was destroyed as an indirect retaliation for the final defeat of Islam in Spain. The Jews are still there. They make some of the finest silver jewelry to be found in the desert. Even now, up and down the Saoura and Zousfana valleys, if you ask a native what language he speaks, he will answer: "Zenati."

An often-repeated statement, no matter how incorrect, takes a long time to disappear from circulation. Thus, the popular misconception of the Sahara as a vast region of sand across which Arabs travel in orderly caravans, from one white-domed city to another, still prevails. A generalization much nearer to the truth would be to say that it is an area of rugged mountains, bare valleys and flat, stony wasteland, sparsely dotted with Negro villages of mud. The sand in the Sahara, according to data supplied by the Geographical Service of the French Army, covers only about a tenth of its surface, and the Arabs, most of them shopkeepers from the north and nomadic traders, form a small percentage of the stationary population. The vast majority of the inhabitants are of Berber (native North African) and/or Negro (native West African) stock. But, the Negroes of today are not those who originally peopled the desert. The latter never took kindly to the colonial designs of the Arabs and the Islamised Berbers; and over the centuries they beat a constant retreat toward the southeast until only a vestige of their society remains, in the region known as the Tibesti. They were replaced by the more docile Soudanese, imported from the south as slaves to work the continuously expanding series of oases.

Tinerhir—spices in the market

In the Sahara, the oasis—which is to say, the forest of date palms—is primarily a man-made affair, and can continue its existence only if the work of irrigating its terrain is kept up unrelentingly. When the Arabs arrived in Africa, twelve centuries ago, they began a project of land reclamation which, if the Europeans continue it with the aid of modern machinery, will transform much of the Sahara into a great, fertile garden. Wherever there was a sign of vegetation, the water was there not far below; it merely needed to be brought to the surface. The Arabs set to work digging wells, constructing reservoirs, building networks of canals along the surface of the ground and systems of subterranean water galleries deep in the earth.

For all these important projects, the recently arrived colonizers needed great numbers of workers who could bear the climate and the malaria that is still endemic in the oases. Soudanese slaves seemed to be the ideal solution, and the latter came to constitute the larger part of the sedentary population of the desert. Each Arab tribe traveled about among the oases it controlled, collecting the produce. It was never the practice or intention of the sons of Allah to live there. They have a saying which goes: "No one lives in the Sahara if he is able to live anywhere else." Slavery has, of course, been abolished officially by the French, but only recently, within our time. Probably the principal blow in the reduction of Timbuktu from its status of capital of the Sahara to its present abject condition, was the closing of the slave market there. But the Sahara, which started out as a Negro country, is still a Negro country, and will probably remain so.

The oases, those magnificent palm groves, are the blood and bone of the desert; life in the Sahara would be unthinkable without them. Wherever human beings are found, an oasis is sure to be nearby. Sometimes the town is surrounded by the trees, but usually it is built just outside, so that none of the fertile ground will be wasted on mere living quarters. The size of an oasis is reckoned by the number of trees it contains, not by the number of square miles it covers, just as the taxes are based on the number of date-bearing trees, not on the amount of land. The prosperity of a region is in direct proportion to the number and size of its oases, some of which are very large. The one at Figuig, for instance, has more than two hundred thousand bearing palms, and the one at Timimoun is forty miles long, with irrigation systems that are of an unbelievable complexity.

To stroll in a Saharan oasis is rather like taking a walk through a well-kept Eden. The alleys are clean, bordered on each side by hand-patted mud walls, not too high to prevent you from seeing the riot of verdure within. Under the high waving palms are the smaller trees—pomegranate, orange, fig, almond. Below these, in neat squares surrounded by narrow ditches or running water, are the vegetables and wheat. No matter how far from the town you stray, you have the same impression of cleanliness, order and insistence on utilizing every square inch of ground. When you come to the edge of the oasis, you find that it is always in the process of being enlarged. Plots of young palms extend out into the glaring desert. Thus far they are useless, but in a few years they will begin to bear, and eventually this sun-blistered land will be a part of the green belt of gardens.

There are a good many birds living in the oases, but their songs and plumage are not appreciated by the inhabitants. The birds eat the young shoots and dig up the seeds as fast as they are planted, and every man and boy carries a slingshot. I traveled through the Sahara with a parrot, four years ago; everywhere the poor bird was glowered at by the natives, and in Timimoun a delegation of three natives came to the hotel one afternoon and suggested that I stop leaving its cage outside the window; otherwise there was no telling what its fate might be. "Nobody likes birds here," they said meaningfully.

It is a custom to build little summerhouses out in the oasis. There is often an element of play and fantasy in the architecture of these edifices which makes them completely captivating. They are small, toy palaces of mud. Here, men have tea with their families at the close of day, or spend the

Above: El Jorf—the town walls

Left: Skoura—in the old fortified village

Above: Erfoud—a rug merchant

Following pages: Tinerhir—a shrine in the old fortified village

night, when it is unusually hot in the town, or invite their friends for a game of *ronda* and a little music. If a man asks you to visit him in his summerhouse, the experience is invariably worth the long walk to get there. You will have to drink at least the three traditional glasses of tea, and you may have to eat a good many almonds and smoke some kif, but it will be cool, there will be the gurgle of running water and the smell of mint in the air, and your host will doubtless bring out a flute. In 1947 I priced one of these houses that had particularly struck my fancy. With its garden and pool, the cost was the equivalent of sixty dollars. The catch was that the owner wanted to retain the right to work the land, because it was unthinkable that it should cease to be productive.

Even though people of dissimilar origins may behave alike in everyday life, the differences immediately become apparent on festive observances. In the M'Zab, which is a purely Arab settlement, it would be inconceivable for the women to take part in a celebration; they stay on the roofs where Arab women belong, and yodel occasionally for the men who are dancing below in the street, contorting themselves in the frenetic, self-immolating dance of the dervish. I once spent an entire night in Ghardaia watching a dozen men dance themselves into unconsciousness beside a bonfire of palm branches. Two burly guards were necessary to prevent them from throwing themselves into the flames. After each man had been heaved back from the fire several times, he finally ceased making his fantastic skyward leaps, staggered and sank to the ground. He was immediately carried outside the circle and covered with blankets, his place being taken by a fresh adept. There was no music or singing, but there were eight drummers, each one playing an instrument of a different size.

In other places, the dance is similar to the Berber *aouache* of the Moroccan Atlas. The participants form a great circle holding hands, women alternating with men, their movements are measured, never frantic, and, although the trance is constantly suggested, it seems never to be arrived at collectively. In the performances I have seen, there has always been a woman in the center with her head and neck hidden by a cloth. She sings and dances, and the chorus around her responds antiphonally. It is all very sedate and low-pitched, but the irrational seems never very far away, perhaps because of the hypnotic effect of the slowly beaten, deep-toned drums.

By far the most interesting single group of Saharan inhabitants is that of the Tuareg, an ancient offshoot of the Kabyle Berbers of Algeria. These people, inappreciative of the "civilizing mission" of the Roman legions, decided to put a thousand or more miles of desert between themselves and their would-be oppressors. They went straight south until they came to a land that seemed to promise them privacy, and there they remained throughout the centuries, their own masters, almost until today. Through all the centuries of Arab domination of the surrounding regions, the Tuareg remained masters of the Hoggar, that immense plateau in the very center of the Sahara, whose highest rocks reach above the nine-thousand-foot line. Their traditional hatred of the Arabs, however, does not appear to have been powerful enough to keep them from becoming partially Islamized, although they are by no means a completely Moslem people. Far from being a piece of property only somewhat more valuable than a sheep, woman has an extremely important place in Tuareg society. The line of succession is purely maternal. Here, it is the men who must be veiled day and night, the women are uncovered. The veil is of fine black gauze, and is worn, so they explain, to protect the soul. But since soul and breath to them are identical, it is not difficult to find a physical explanation. The excessive dryness of the atmosphere often causes disturbances in the nasal passages. The veil conserves the breath's moisture, is a sort of little air-conditioning plant, and this helps keep out the evil spirits which otherwise would manifest their presence by making the nostrils bleed, a common ailment in this part of the world.

It is scarcely fair to refer to these proud people as Tuareg. The word is a term of opprobrium meaning "lost souls," given them by their traditional enemies the Arabs, but one which, in the outside world, has stuck. They call themselves *Imochagh*, the free ones. Among all the Berber-speaking peoples, the Tuareg are the only ones to have devised a system of writing their language. No one knows how long their alphabet has been in use, but it is a true phonetical alphabet, quite as well planned and logical as the Roman, with twenty-three simple and thirteen compound letters.

Unfortunately for them, the Tuareg have never been able to get on among themselves. Internecine warfare has gone on unceasingly for centuries. Until the French military put a stop to it, it had been a common practice for one tribe to set out on plundering expeditions against a neighboring tribe. During these voyages, the wives of the absent men remained faithful to their husbands, the strict Targui moral code recommending death as a punishment for infidelity. However, a married woman whose husband is away is free to go at night to the graveyard dressed in her finest apparel, lie on the tombstone of one of her ancestors, and invoke a certain spirit called Idebni, who always appears in the guise of one of the young men of the community. If she can win Idebni's favor, he will give her news of her husband, if not, he strangles her. The Tuareg women, being very clever, always manage to bring news of their husbands from the cemetery.

Twenty-five years ago (the first motor crossing of the Sahara was accomplished in 1923) it was still a matter of months to get from, say, Touggourt to Zinder, or from the Tafilalet to Gao. In 1934, I was in Erfoud inquiring about caravans to Timbuktu. Yes, they said, one was leaving in a few weeks; it would take from sixteen to twenty weeks. How would I get back? The caravan would probably set out on its return trip at this time next year. They were surprised to see that this information lessened my interest. How could you expect to do it more quickly?

Of course, the proper way to travel in the Sahara is by camel, particularly if you're a good walker, since after about two hours of the camel's motion you are glad to get down and walk for four. Each succeeding day is likely to bring with it a greater percentage of time spent off the camel. Nowadays, if you like, you can leave Algiers in the morning by plane, and be fairly well into the desert by evening, but the traveler who gives in to this temptation, like the reader of a mystery story who skips through the book to arrive at the solution quickly, deprives himself of most of the pleasure of the journey. The practical means of locomotion here today, for the person who wants to see something, is the trans-Saharan truck, a compromise between camel and airplane.

There are only two trails across the desert at present (the Piste Imperiale through Mauretania not being open to the public) and I should not recommend either to drivers of private automobiles. The trucks, on the other hand, are especially built for the region. If there is any sort of misadventure, the wait is not likely to be more than twenty-four hours, since the truck is expected at the next town, and there is always an ample supply of water aboard. But the lone car that gets stuck in the Sahara is in trouble.

Usually, you can go to the fort of any town and telephone ahead to the next post, asking them to notify the hotelkeeper there of your intended arrival. However, should the lines be down, there is no way of assuring yourself a room in advance, save by mail, which is extremely slow. Unless you travel with your own blankets this can be a serious drawback, as the hotels are small, often having only half a dozen rooms, and the winter nights are cold. The temperature goes to several degrees below freezing, reaching its lowest point just before dawn. The same courtyard that may show 125° when it is flooded with sun at two in the afternoon, will register only 28° the following morning. So, it is good to know you are going to have a room and a bed in your next stopping place. Not that there is heating of any sort in the hotels, but by keeping the window shut you can help the thick mud walls conserve some of the daytime heat. Even so, I have awakened to find a sheet of ice over the water in the glass beside my bed.

These violent extremes of temperature are due, of course, to the dryness of the atmosphere, whose relative humidity is often less than 5 per cent. When you reflect that the soil often attains a temperature of 175° F. during the summer, you can understand that the principal consideration in planning

streets and houses should be that of keeping out as much light as possible. Light and heat are synonymous. The streets are kept dark by building them underneath and inside the houses, and the houses have no windows in the massive walls. The French have introduced windows in many of their buildings, but these open onto wide, vaulted arcades, and thus, while they give air, they let in little light. The result, everywhere in the Sahara, is that once you are out of the sun you live in a Stygian gloom.

Even in the Sahara there is no spot where rain has not been known to fall, and its arrival is an event that calls for celebration—drumming, dancing, firing of guns. The storms are violent and unpredictable. Considering their disastrous effects, one wonders that the people can welcome them with such unmixed emotions. Enormous walls of water rush down the dry river beds, pushing everything before them and isolating the towns. The roofs

Rissani—the marketplace

125

of the houses cave in, and often the walls themselves. A prolonged rain would destroy every town in the Sahara, since the *tob*, of which everything is built, is softer than our adobe.

In 1932 I decided to spend the winter in the M'Zab of Southern Algeria. The rattletrap bus started out from Laghouat at night in a heavy rain. Not far to the south, the trail crossed a flat stretch about a mile wide, slightly lower than the surrounding country. Even as we were in it, the water began to rise around us, and in a moment the motor died. The passengers jumped out and waded about in water that was soon up to their waists; in all directions there were dim white figures in burnooses moving slowly through the flood, like storks. They were looking for a shallow route back to dry land, but they did not find it. In the end they carried me, the only European in the party, all the way to Laghouat on their backs, leaving the bus and the luggage to drown out there in the rain. When I got to Ghardaia two days later, the rain (which was the first in seven years) had made a deep pond along an embankment the French had built for the trail. Such an enormous quantity of water all in one place was a source of great wonder to the inhabitants. For days there was a constant procession of women coming to carry it away in jugs. The children tried to walk on its surface, and two small ones were drowned. Ten days later the water had almost disappeared. A thick, brilliant green froth covered what was left, but the women continued to come with their jugs, pushing aside the scum and taking what remained. For once, they were able to collect as much water as they could store in their houses. Ordinarily it was a rather expensive commodity that they had to buy each morning from the town watersellers, who brought it in from the oasis.

Most of the towns are better supplied with water than Ghardaia was then. But the quality of the water varies greatly, and the traveler does well to look into the matter at each new place before drinking.

Although the water has been known to cause illness and occasionally death, it is primarily the lack of it which one needs to fear. Generally speaking, it is impossible to have too much of it with you. People still die of thirst in the Sahara, so take along, on every stage of the journey, far more than you can imagine you would need. Then, if you hear strange explosions and groans among the rocks, you will know it is only a result of the sudden shifts in temperature, and not the laughter of Roul, the *djinn* who comes to watch the thirsty traveler in his death agonies.

There are probably few accessible places on the face of the globe where you can get less comfort for more money. In the past two years the prices in dollars have more than quintupled, and the accommodations are as miserable as ever. You can still get something flat to lie down on, stewed turnips and sand, noodles and jam, and a few tendons of something euphemistically called chicken to eat, and the stub of a candle to undress by at night, but you will pay five times what you did in 1949 for these things, which is to say, your bill will now be about three dollars a day in the smaller places, and double that in the larger ones. Inasmuch as you must carry your own food and stove with you in any case, it sometimes seems scarcely worth while to bother with the "meals" provided by the hotels. But, if you depend entirely on your canned goods they give out too quickly. Everything gives out eventually anyway— your coffee, tea, sugar, cigarettes—and you settle down to a life devoid of these luxuries, using a pile of soiled clothing as a pillow for your head at night and a burnoose for a blanket.

Perhaps the logical question at this point is: Why go? The answer is that once you have been there you can't help yourself. Once you have fallen victim to the spell of this vast, luminous, silent country, no other place is quite strong enough for you, no other surroundings can provide the supremely satisfying sensation of existing in the midst of something that is absolute. You will go back, whatever the cost in discomfort and dollars, for the absolute has no price.

Rissani—a Tuareg merchant

Eastern Sahara, oasis of Merzouga—desert tribesmen at the walls of an inn